D1534806

A Woman of
Interest

A WOMAN OF INTEREST

June 2013

Michelle
Strong, Independent, Women
Yes!

By Cindy Zimmermann

Hugs & More Hugs,
Cindy

Cover Design by Neiger Design
Edited by Barbara Toombs
Book Design by The Printed Page

ISBN 978-0-9886080-0-9

Manufactured in the United States of America

Published by WIS Global, LLC
P. O. Box 44005 Phoenix, Arizona 85064
www.awomanofinterest.com

Books are available in quantity for promotional or premium use.

Library of Congress Cataloging

Zimmermann, Cindy.
    A woman of interest / by Cindy Zimmermann. -- Phoeniz, Ariz. : WIS
    Global, c2012.
        p. ; cm.
        ISBN: 978-0-9886080-0-9
        Summary: In heartfelt letters to her friend, Hollywood legend
Ken Rotcop, Cindy Zimmermann writes her true-life memoirs of a seemingly perfect life torn to shreds. She shares her public and private turmoil as she became the target of one allegation after another, year after year as she struggled to maintain and reconstruct her life—a life shattered through murder, divorce, estate disputes and her family torn apart. Cindy shares her letters as a thank-you note to her family, friends, and the professionals who helped her. Additionally important to her is the opportunity to share with her readers what she has come to learn: whether used for good or evil, never understimate the power of the handwritten word.--Publisher.
        1. Zimmermann, Cindy. 2. Murder--Investigation--Arizona--
Scottsdale. 3. Evidence, Documentary--Arizona--Scottsdale--Case
studies. 4. Writing--Identification--Case studies. 5. Letter writing--
Psychological aspects. 6. Murder victims' families--Psychological
aspects--Personal narratives. 7. Family crises--Personal
narratives. 8. Divorce--Psychological aspects--Personal narratives.
9. Murder--Psychological aspects--Personal narratives.
10. Friendship--Psychological aspects. 11. Gratitude--Personal
narratives. I. Rotcop, Ken. II. Title.
HV6533.A6 Z56 2012
364.152/30979173--dc23   1212

CONTENTS

FOREWORD

Condensed from the Arizona Republic, July 21, 2008

SCOTTSDALE – Strangulation and gunshot wounds caused the death of 50-year-old Paul Zimmermann, whose disappearance earlier this month sparked a probe into a bizarre murder-suicide case.

Scottsdale police found Zimmermann's tarp-wrapped body last week in a vacant lot. He had been shot in the torso.

His family reported him missing on July 12.

After finding the victim's car two days later, police developed information that led them to the home of Tom Sullivan, 55.

When officers asked Sullivan for identification, he disappeared into his house and shot and killed himself.

A man is murdered. His killer commits suicide. End of story.

Hardly.

For there were those who believed that somehow Paul Zimmermann's wife was responsible for her husband's death. I mean, what are the odds that on the day that the man was murdered, his divorce from his wife became finalized?

Something wasn't right.

The police called Cindy Zimmermann "a person of interest." She was brought in, interrogated, and suspected.

But of what?

When I met Cindy, she was looking for someone to write her side of the story. I told her she should write it herself.

"But how?" she asked. "How do I start?"

"Write it in the form of a long letter to me," I suggested. "Stream of conscience. Just tell me everything that happened from when you first met Paul and into the turbulent days following his death. Send me at least 20 pages a week."

And so she did.

In her own words, with memories as vivid as today's headlines, here is her story…as told to me by Cindy Zimmermann.

Ken Rotcop
Woodland Hills, CA
August 21, 2012

PREFACE

I am often asked, "Why Ken Rotcop? How did Ken get you to write?" It's true I had others who tried to help me. But for some reason, the time, the person, weren't right.

I met Ken Rotcop at an Artist-in-Residence Dinner at Lon's at The Hermosa Inn in Paradise Valley, Arizona. Ken has become my "pen pal" of sorts, the person who has kept me writing and writing. For some reason, he thought someone might be interested in reading my story. Ken Rotcop, WGA award-winning writer, author and former creative head of Embassy Pictures, Hanna-Barbera, Cannon Films, and Trans-World Productions—all extraordinary accomplishments, but to me, for me, he has become a dear, trusted friend.

Initially I sent a box of papers to Ken and said, "Here, *you* can write it."

Ken returned the box and said, "Cindy, no one can write this but you. Will you commit to writing 20 pages every week? Write to me in a letter form, that's where you are most comfortable. I will ask you questions to lead you."

Truth be told, I didn't even want to write "it." I wanted to write my column for Pen World magazine, handwrite letters to my friends, write in my journals, write in my children's baby books, write my holiday letters. But these would not be the only paths my writing would take.

For some reason, Ken made me feel comfortable that he understood and respected my life as I experienced it. He would honor what I honor. With this reassurance, I began to write.

There are sure to be details recalled by others that differ from mine. But in the end, what matters most to me is that this to be the longest thank-you note ever written to those I treasure, to those who have been a part of my life. And as a reader of my story, we have now become a part of each other's lives.

So I write.

Dear Ken...

AND SO IT BEGINS

Dear Ken,

Never in a million years. Never.

If you ever thought this could happen to the father of my children, you did not know him. Never in a million years.

Paul was known for being tough, aware of his surroundings, able to protect himself, and quick—maybe too quick—to protect himself and those he cared about. That a man weighing less than 90 pounds would kill him speaks volumes on just how different Paul was in the last months of his life when compared to the man I had married in 1986.

But to understand how we got to this point, I must first look back.

Maybe it's best to start with your question—and it's a question I am asked often—"What about the men in your life?" I'm struggling, Ken. Because surely you know by now that whatever you ask me, my answer will be what I want to write about and not necessarily the answer to your question! Trust me, I know where you were trying to go with your question, but that's not where I want to go—at least, not yet. So I will start at the beginning instead.

Like most everyone, the first man in life was my father. I was blessed. My father adored me and I adored him. I was his 21st birthday gift. I was born on the 4th of July, his birthday. He taught me how to celebrate and love life.

I don't recall my father saying many cross words to me. He didn't say many cross words to anyone. He would just move on to something else or act like he didn't hear you. He had a wonderful sense of humor. We were as different as night and day. I think I entertained him, or at least I tried to. A simple man, he worked for the railroad his entire career. My love of fancy things entertained him. Most people loved Richie.

I am grateful the last words my father spoke to me were, "I love you, sweetie." It was Thanksgiving Day. I had cooked for him. I had taken the time to leave our home full of guests to walk him to his car. My last words to him were, "I love you, too, Daddy." My father and I did not talk to each other in this fashion. It seemed odd even at the time. He died that night. My father would like it that I can laugh. He wouldn't want me to be upset, yet surely he knows I was. I will always miss him.

With my father's death, I learned a valuable lesson about parting comments. They may very well be our last; in fact, every word could be our last. We tend to spend a great deal of energy on the "firsts," when it's the "last" that usually becomes most poignant. I read that somewhere long ago and it's stuck with me.

My father would like the irony that when I flew back to Kansas City with his body for the funeral, I was in first class, and his remains were in cargo. He would laugh that I carried many, many books with me to prepare his eulogy. He wouldn't mind that I got very tipsy on the free wine served. He wouldn't mind that I cried on the plane because I was so upset.

My father's eulogy was important to me. I wanted to get it just right. I remember my husband Paul saying it was one of my best public speeches, and his only regret was that he hadn't thought to have it recorded. He spoke of this regret often. He couldn't think of everything; he was grieving the loss of my father as well. They had a fond respect for each other. When teasing each other over one of my latest escapades, Paul would say to my father, "She's your daughter." Dad would respond, "You married her!"

My father would, however, mind that I spent a month in bed watching his funeral video over and over again. Crying and crying.

The second man in my life was my younger brother, Robert Kirk. Only 18 months apart, we have always been very close and remain so to this day. I cannot imagine life without him. I cannot even begin to put into words how much Robert has done for me and for my children. Actually, I think anyone who knows him thinks he has done a lot for them, too. He's just a person who gives and gives. Somehow, in some way, *every* way, he has been a hands-on uncle for the kids, a hands-on brother and friend to me. I am at a loss for words to describe my gratitude for all he has done.

But I know your question, Ken, was directed more towards romantic "relationships," wasn't it?

Mike Mulcahy was my first true romantic love. We were very much in love—so much so, we decided to get married. Getting married at 18 is rarely a good idea. Really what we did was "play house." What else do you know how to do when you're 18? But I loved him. I loved him very much. And he loved me. He read John Steinbeck books. He loved poetry. Isn't it funny that's what I remember most about him? Honestly, I thought it was sexy. I still do. A man that reads and writes, very sexy! Oh, and he was handsome. Of course, we were passionately attracted to each other. However, it didn't take but two years for me to realize this wasn't a good decision, this getting married stuff. I wanted a divorce.

At that point in my life, I decided to focus on work, perhaps a career. I have always loved to learn. I am, by nature, curious. Education has always been an important part of my life. I also love to make money. Sometimes one would take precedent over the other in my life.

So here I was, in my early twenties, and I got a job as a secretary and took it by storm. I was promoted into a sales position that would have normally required a college degree. I did very well financially, had a company car, and an expense account! This was big heady stuff for someone of my tender age. I soon realized

I was going to need a college degree to go hand-in-hand with work experience in order to move forward—that and an attitude adjustment. I learned that if you yell, "Fuck You!" at one of your bosses, you tend to get fired. Funny how that works. So then I was unemployed, taking college classes.

Well, not exactly unemployed. I was waitressing, a skill for which I am grateful and on which I can always rely. But after paying my dues of waitressing, being humbled a bit, and completing my associate degree, I got a medical sales job with Acme United in my hometown of Kansas City. I was thrilled.

Naturally, the working world brought a whole new selection of men into my life. I had the pleasure of working for a man named Randy Blackwell, who was a star salesman in Kansas City. Everybody loved him. He was promoted to sales manager, and I was interviewed for his position. They were big shoes to step into. But from my perspective we were a great team. He helped me learn the ropes. I respected his well-deserved legacy. He went on to be a great leader for Acme United, and we became personal and professional friends, playing soccer and softball together. Our families liked each other as well.

My personal challenge, however, was that although Mike and I had both agreed to the divorce, we couldn't seem to detach. We kept seeing each other and couldn't seem to break apart. I knew I needed to get away for a fresh start.

I remember the spring of 1984, when about the fifth Sunday softball game was rained out and rescheduled. I thought to myself, "Why do I live in Kansas City?" I was ready to move on. I found a book that evaluated cities around the country based on economics, weather, education, standard of living, and so forth. I highlighted things I liked and disliked. Phoenix, Arizona, seemed to be just the place for me. I was going to move to Phoenix.

Because Randy and I were friends, I had mentioned my new goal of relocating to him. He asked me if I was moving to Phoenix to leave Acme or just wanted to move. I told him I wanted to move to Phoenix, but loved Acme. As luck would have it, the sales representative in Phoenix was resigning. I could move to Phoenix *and* keep my job. I was thrilled yet again. Acme paid for my move. I got settled and continued my professional success in Phoenix.

I was in Denver, Colorado, on business for Acme, when I received the phone call. At the age of 24, Mike Mulcahy, my first husband, had died. Tragically, he had fallen while standing on the floorboard on the outside of a Volkswagen Bug. It seems he and his girlfriend, ironically by the name of Cindy, had been in a disagreement. Known for his hot temper, he insisted she let him out of the car. When she refused, he opened the door while the car was still moving, and stood on the floorboard. He lost his balance, fell, and died instantly from a head injury.

His parents called me with this news. They knew I would want to know. They knew I still cared about him as a person, as a friend. They asked if I would come home for his funeral. "Of course, I will get the next flight," I replied.

I was treated like family some four years later. They wanted me in the family. I wanted to be with them. I was so very sorry for what had happened to Mike. He was a dear man. You can see now, Ken, why I never wanted to get married again. First, it doesn't work. Then the man dies. It's a lot to handle when you're in your early twenties—or at any age, for that matter.

Unfortunately, by this time, all was not well with Acme United. Our product line was coming under fire from various competitors. The writing was on the wall. Commissions and market share were eroding quickly. Fortunately, I had great relationships with my local American Hospital Supply Representatives. I had earned a reputation for being creative in my marketing slash selling. The reps brought to my attention that a territory was opening up with a company called Tecnol. Did I want to interview, they asked me? Of course! One hitch: Tecnol was headquartered in Dallas, Texas, and had never hired a female sales representative before.

They were known for their male salesmen, how much money they made, and how bright the future of the company was. They were also known for their creative gold standard marketing ideas. There were stock options available. It was a golden opportunity, well known in the industry.

My American Hospital Supply friends secured an interview for me. It probably was a token interview. But I surprised the Tecnol team during my interview with how well I knew the Phoenix- and Denver-based sales people. They wanted me to get the job. I flew to Dallas for more interviews.

It was an interesting time for a woman to go on an interview back in the 1980s. On one hand, I thought to myself, I could make a fuss about the inappropriate questions they asked me. Or, I could get the job and prove that females—at least *this* female—could be a superstar.

I got the job. I was thrilled. In order to show my appreciation, I sent out bottles of champagne to everyone who helped me land the position. As I recall, I sent out 15 bottles of champagne. It took a lot of convincing for a Texas cowboy to understand this 5'2" 110-pound sales lady!

I want to be very clear as I write about my years with Tecnol that I am very, very grateful for the opportunity to work there. It is my intention to write of a time in history when females were finding their way into unconventional positions. Companies were trying to navigate the new demands of being profitable, yet wanted to incorporate family values into their cultures. If my writing gives you any other impression, it is absolutely inaccurate.

From the beginning, as I recall, I was successful in selling Tecnol products, which I loved, and had the relationships in the territory to be a success almost from the get-go. I worked for a man named Tommy Mann. He was a great guy, too.

There are good and bad things about being successful right from the beginning. One, it's great to be a success. Two, it pisses the boys off. They didn't like me winning. It was a love/hate relationship. The numbers were there to prove my sales, but numbers can be interpreted in many ways. Maybe I hadn't learned as much about humility as I needed to.

I had an unfortunate sales meeting and reaction to an awards banquet. From my perspective, I had won the sales rep of the year award. Tecnol management felt that four of us had won. I was furious. I didn't want to share my coveted award with three other people—especially those who hadn't even made sales plan. It all seems so silly and petty now, but at the time I was very upset about it.

In my fury, I burned a few bridges that were probably never repaired. I was learning how to win friends and influence people. It's not about getting too attached to any prizes. Especially when you're making a lot of money, the potential for a lot more, everyday responsibilities were everything I dreamed of and, other than a sales meeting now and then, I needed to let some shit go.

I was fortunate Tommy Mann was a great mentor and he told me just this: "Cindy, enjoy your life, get over the award. Move forward." And I did.

I didn't want to get married again. It was not a secret. After the heartbreak of my first marriage, my first true love, I never wanted to go through that pain again. I loved being single. I loved my career. I loved my freedom. Then I met Paul.

Casper, Wyoming, 1985. We were attracted to each other from the first moment we met at a medical product fair in a hospital. Who would have thought?

Paul was well-educated, a gentleman, classy, hard-working, hard-playing, handsome. Everything a girl could want. We had great fun at the after-event party with our mutual business colleagues. The next day he returned to Denver, Colorado. I returned to Phoenix, Arizona.

There were a dozen red roses from Paul waiting for me. He was generous, thoughtful, and romantic. He treated me like a queen. It was no wonder "Caribbean Queen" by Billy Ocean became our song. I can't begin to count the number of times we danced to that. Paul was not much inclined to dance, but he did, to please me, as I did things to please him. Relationships are funny that way. What begins as acts of love somehow turn into compromises, which can turn into a life one doesn't even recognize, don't you think?

Everybody wanted to meet this "Paul guy." Who was this man who had caught my eye? Yes, it was Paul Zimmermann, and we were happy. He had an opportunity to move to Chicago, and wanted me to go with him. I asked Tecnol if they had a territory for me. Fortunately, they *created* a territory. This was good news and bad news as well, because they rearranged a well-loved guy's territory to make room for me, and my territory location was perceived as better than his. He and a lot of the old guard at Tecnol were upset. I ruffled more feathers, but kept on producing.

On the home front, Paul and I lived together for about six months in Highland Park, Illinois, before becoming engaged. We had a beautiful wedding in West Palm Beach, Florida, and then started to think about a family. It wasn't good news for Tecnol. They weren't excited about females, babies, leaves of absence, and so forth. This was all new—in fact, it really was new for the culture of America. I was right in the middle of it. Story of my life.

The announcement of my first pregnancy was met with little excitement at Tecnol. As I recall, I waited quite a while into my pregnancy to make the announcement.

You know, there are moments in time you will remember forever. We were at home, watching a Kansas City Royals baseball game on television, and I felt slight discomfort, just a tummy ache; no big deal. I'd gotten up to go to the restroom. Something had fallen in the toilet. I was innocent. This was my first baby. I knew nothing. I thought you got pregnant, had a baby, that's it. We called my ob-gyn just to be sure. He wanted us to come to the hospital right away. He wasn't innocent; he knew I was in trouble. Calmly, he insisted that we come. The doctor had suggested we keep track of my "pains" on the drive over. Lake Zurich was a good 30-minute drive to the hospital in Evanston. I was having my "pains" every two minutes. We had no idea. I lay down in the back seat on my left side like he had told me.

We got to the hospital, and that's when things started to take on a life of their own. Suddenly, I was being rushed around. Paul and I were separated, so he could sign papers. We both had worked in hospitals our entire careers, so we were used to the environment.

Reality struck when the doctor said, "You're having the baby tonight." I was 26-1/2 weeks pregnant. This could not be. I told the doctors, "No, give me Terbutaline, the medicine that stops the contractions."

"No, it is too late," the doctor said.

I insisted, "Please give it to me."

The doctor said, "No, it is too risky, Cindy, you could have a heart attack." He would not give me the drug. Heart attack, broken heart…aren't they one and the same?

Ok, so we moved on to Plan B. We would have our baby and everything would be wonderful. The doctors and nurses began to educate us about surfactant, early-term lung development or lack thereof, in our sweet baby Brian's case. We were fortunate the Evanston hospital was part of a trial for a new drug that had proved very promising in lung development of premature babies. We were asked whether we wanted Brian to participate in the trial, take the medicine. Of course, absolutely. You see, everything was going to be okay.

So, another new man came into my life: Brian Paul was born on September 1, 1986. He was tiny, but we thought we had the resources, the medical powers to make him healthy, wealthy, and wise. He was…for about six hours. During these six hours, the nurses began to care for my post-delivery body and prepare Paul and me for parenting our new baby. We were gently educated about the extended hospital stay Brian would need. He would probably be in the hospital for three months. He would need a great deal of care. The nurses and doctors in the neonatal ICU are trained to guide parents. They are angels; I know for sure.

Like all patients, you begin to listen very closely for the steps of a professional to bring the latest good news of improvement and healing to your room. The first news of change was not good. Brian had had a seizure. He was blind. I remember Paul and I processing this information, but being eternal optimists, we came to see it as a setback, but not the end of the world. Okay, I would quit my job and drive him to the school for the blind. He would be fine. Again, we had resources to make him healthy, wealthy, and wise.

What we did not know is what the doctors knew. The medicine wasn't working. Surfactant was not being made for his little lungs. Brian would be the exception to the high percentage of babies that responded to the trial. As I recall, it was in the 80th or 90th percentile of success.

The next time the medical team visited our room, the news was worse. Brian had had a severe brain hemorrhage. He was severely mentally retarded. Severely. The medical team gave Paul and me time to get used to this new development. There was no way this could be good news.

Then they came back in the room and had the real talk. We needed to take Brian off of the machines that were keeping his little body alive. He wasn't going to make it. We needed to sign the papers to end our dear son's life on Earth. We were devastated.

In less than 24 hours, I was no longer pregnant. Our son had gone to heaven. We went home to our house.

We were devastated beyond belief. Our friends and family were devastated for us. We had called friends and family to tell them our happy news when Brian was born. Then the very next day we had to make the calls to tell our friends and family that our baby had died.

I came to learn many years later from Amy Irwin, a friend in the pharmaceutical industry, that most likely Brian got the placebo in the study. A placebo never crossed our minds. For years, Paul and I wondered why the drug didn't work for Brian.

Paul and I made the decision to have Brian Paul buried beside his grandmother in New Jersey. Though I had never met her, it gave Paul and me comfort that somehow she would be looking after Brian in heaven and laying next to him here on Earth.

Paul and I were given grief counseling by our medical team. This type of loss can be devastating to a marriage, we were told. Most couples (high 90th percentile) divorce after losing a child. The loss is so great to heal individually, it is even greater to heal as a couple. Paul and I were always very aware of these odds. We were determined to beat them.

We created our own tradition of remembering Brian. I always wore a sapphire ring, his birthstone, to remember Brian at our family celebrations. We would try to speak of him to keep his spirit alive. We raised our children to understand they have a brother in heaven.

Life must go on. Slowly but surely we went back to work, we went back to life. It was not easy. Somehow Paul and I decided it would be a good idea for me to take a class at Roosevelt University. A class would give me a fresh place to go without the reminders of my pregnancy, our son, our tremendous grief.

The fist night I went to class I walked into the room to see one of my neonatal nurses in my class. I began to cry. I would never be able to escape this heartache. She hugged and held me. She reassured me that Paul and I, our marriage, would be okay. Of all the couples she had worked with, she told me she had never seen two people care so much for each other. She had never witnessed such respectful conversation, educated dialogue about the care of a family.

She was right. That's how we were. But nonetheless, I went home to tell Paul I couldn't take the class. I couldn't see our nurse every week. Of course, he understood and agreed. My lesson wasn't from the teacher, it was from our nurse. I am grateful for her positive reflections of our marriage and our parenting of Brian Paul. I am grateful for Brian's sign from heaven that we were going to be okay. He would help us.

Back to work. Tecnol was very supportive, generous, and understanding. It wasn't a heartless company, just a company driven for profit, as it should be. They needed their "Tecnol Tiger," as I referred to myself, to get back to work. I needed to get back to being a Tecnol Tiger, too.

It wouldn't be long before we decided to have another baby. We were advised to wait a year. We needed to heal emotionally and myself physically. But we trusted ourselves. I wasn't a spring chicken, getting ready to enter my thirties soon. We waited just a few months before I was pregnant again.

My pregnancies weren't going to be easy. I had been diagnosed with an incompetent cervix. It's not really funny, but it kind of makes me chuckle. You don't know how many people have said to me, "Cindy, what is an incompetent cervix? Who has an incompetent cervix? Only *you* would have something like that."

Simply put, an incompetent cervix means there was too much pressure on my body and it would go into premature labor. With a cerclage (a thick metal stitch to sew my cervix shut) and bed rest, the possibility of my body not going into pre-term labor was greatly improved. I had to be on bed rest for five months for each child and use high-risk pregnancy doctors with a close medical watch. There were pumps, new drugs, or treatments with each pregnancy.

They were a long five months each time I was pregnant. Paul did the best he could to be supportive and at the same time handle his responsibilities as the president of Baxter Physical Therapy. He seemed to do it all effortlessly. Not one to complain, he was excited for us to have a family. He loved being the leader of a cutting-edge, high-quality healthcare division. He liked caring for people, especially me. I remember during one of my pregnancies, each day when he got home from work, Paul played Scrabble with me, literally *every* day. I don't know how he did it. But he did. He wanted his

A Woman of Interest

babies so very much. He would always be heartbroken about losing Brian, we both were. But Paul was a bit more shaken by it.

Bed rest and Tecnol didn't go well together. First I moved, then I got pregnant, and after that I was on disability leave for five months. Not good, but they would make do for me. Because of the success of the territory and market at the time, I was able to manage the territory from home while on bed rest without too much confusion in the territory. It's not to say motherhood wasn't dinging up my career. It was. It also didn't set well that Paul was a president for one of the divisions within our partnering company, American Hospital Supply. Again, good news/bad news. Great for some relationships, but could be frustrating as well, to try and manage me with my husband being a president. Hands off. Yet I was really pushing some buttons at Tecnol.

We were thrilled when our oldest son, Joseph Paul, arrived on November 11, 1988. (It was our family tradition for our children to have their middle names be Paul or Cynthia.) We followed doctors' orders to the T. I stayed in bed and tried not to be nervous. Paul tried not to be nervous. But we *were* nervous. After losing our Brian, we were very nervous. Joseph arrived safe and sound. Now we just had to keep him safe and sound here on Earth!

I laugh to myself because truly Paul and I were neurotic. We bought every monitor known to man to make sure Joseph wasn't kidnapped or left unattended. We slept with the baby monitor in our bed, with his bedroom right next to ours, to make sure he was safe; the volume on high just to be sure he *was* safe. We left mounds of directions and rules to be adhered to when we left him in the care of others.

Naturally, I followed the school bus to his first day of kindergarten. I share this with you, Ken, because it's funny and it's precious. All families have these funny, precious memories. The importance of them is that we learn to respect each other for our nuances and further love each other for them.

My son Joe is a very special man. Mrs. DiVito, his kindergarten teacher, even commented on his remarkable nature. She told me a story about how he always helped a fellow classmate, who was disabled. When I casually thanked her for sharing the story with me, she made it a point to explain to me that it was highly unusual for a child of his age to be so empathetic. It was a gift; he is a gift. I am proud he is my son.

After Joe was born, healthy and sound, I returned to work. There was peace for a while, maybe for a couple of years. Then we wanted another baby. This time Tecnol wasn't so thrilled with my bed rest. They weren't thrilled with the continual friction between Paul's division of physical therapy and our orthopedic division. The tension was mounting.

Somewhere in all of this, Tecnol went public. An IPO. It was a big deal. A really big deal. I was part of the road show; part of the company for a good number of the building years. It was just a fantastic financial opportunity for me and my family. The money Paul and I made from this IPO would propel our fortune forward tremendously. Again, good news/bad news.

As with all of my babies, during my pregnancy with Kevin, I was on bed rest. At the appropriate time, the cervical cerclage was taken out and I got up to move around. In theory, the baby was supposed to practically fall out of me. Not Kevin. From the beginning, he had a mind of his own. We all kind of hoped he would be born on the 4th of July, and share a birthday with me and my father. We thought it would be fun to have a three-generation birthday tradition. It didn't happen that way. I was up on my feet for six more weeks, but this little guy wasn't coming out to play. Finally, the doctors had to induce labor, and Kevin arrived healthy on August 7, 1991.

Somehow, Joe had survived our obsessive adulation, but he was thrilled with the arrival of his younger brother. The pressure would finally be off! Being the center of attention can take its toll, I'm sure.

I was determined to be a good mother. In one of the parenting books I read (heaven only knows which one, I read so many), it was suggested that to help older siblings from feeling displaced or left out, a new baby should give his or her siblings a gift. We started this tradition with Kevin, who presented his older brother Joe with a small toy, which he loved.

From the moment he was born, Kevin had a passion for life. He simply loved it. He was happy all the time. He adored his brother Joe. He adored his younger sister Michelle. According to his teachers, from an early age he was physically and mentally gifted. Some of it was innate. Some of it I'm sure came from trying to keep up with his brother and father. The three of them loved to wrestle and play. I must admit the rough-housing made me nervous, but it made my sons tough and competitive. They were taught to play hard and never give up.

It was a difficult decision deciding when to send Kevin to kindergarten. With an August birthday, he would be the youngest in his class, maybe more slight in size, but intellectually and emotionally he was more than ready to go. We decided to send him. I'm sure the decision came with mounds of testing, discussion, more analyzing, graphs, more discussions. I must laugh. Unquestionably, Paul and I took this parenting thing very, very seriously. Yes, I followed his bus to school on *his* first day of kindergarten, too—and yes, the wonderful Mrs. DiVito was his kindergarten teacher as well.

This last time, my leave of absence from Tecnol wasn't met with a lukewarm reception. It was met with a lot of hostility. There were some discussions of a maternity leave lawsuit. It was really ugly. By this time, Paul's career was in full swing. We were traveling internationally for his opportunities.

I'd been back to work about six weeks after delivering Kevin when we had a sales meeting in Hawaii. It was a beautiful sales meeting. Tecnol was known for its over-the-top sales meetings.

They liked to treat their sales and marketing people well. But my heart wasn't in it. I missed my family.

I was tired of carrying the female sales torch, whether self-induced or not. I came to the conclusion in Hawaii that it was time for me to stop working. The crowning moment came when our nanny called to tell me something Joe had done at preschool that day. I thought to myself, "I don't want a nanny calling to tell me about my children." I wanted to be home.

I called Paul and told him I wanted to resign. He was surprised, but thrilled. He really did want a traditional family, even though he had supported me and my career. It was getting a lot to juggle: two demanding careers, two children, and our active social life. On the bus from the hotel to the airport in Hawaii, I told my manager, "I am resigning." As he was also a friend, he understood, but asked me if I was sure. Yes, I was. I resigned my medical sales career, and would not work for a paycheck for the next 20 years.

There were some hard feelings about this as well. Some people felt I had come back to work just to get the free trip to Hawaii. Those rumors were fairly painless to me. As a friend pointed out, Paul and I could more than easily fly to Hawaii; I didn't need a free trip. As always, my friends' loving support could take the sting out of any nasty comment.

Honestly, I was focused on my family. When I close a door, it's closed. I didn't look back and could care less what was thought of my resignation decision. I was happy to be with my family. I am very, very grateful for the opportunities and the people I worked with in the medical world. I consider many, if not most, of them dear friends to this day.

So Joe and Kevin are two tremendously important men in my life, but they were followed by a very important woman in my life: Michelle, born on December 13, 1994. After the months of bed rest, her delivery date was expected and planned. Goes to show you how every good plan can go awry; especially, it seems, in Cindy World. In this last baby I would deliver, somehow the umbilical cord got wrapped around her neck. She was blue and in danger. Because I was medicated, I didn't know the danger she was in. Paul did.

When we were racing down the hallway for an emergency C-section, surrounded by nurses and doctors, he assured me that everything was going to be okay. Thankfully, it was; she was. Paul held his sweet baby girl and adored her every moment of their life together. He played countless hours of Uno, Monopoly, or any other game she wanted to play. He would buy her anything she wanted. Though she wanted little; she has always been gracious and not expecting indulgence. Do I sound like I adore her? Yes, I do. The world is hers, to be certain.

She is one of those young ladies everyone wishes they could be. From the moment she was born, she has been a delight. I remember once her grandmother was taking her for a walk in her stroller. When she returned, her grandmother shared with me that Michelle waved to everyone and everyone waved back. That is my daughter. She is thoughtful, generous, has a really good head on her shoulders, and a great sense of humor. We joke that she is doing a good job of raising me! It's not far from the truth. I am so very grateful for her well-being.

Since education was so important to me, I decided to work on getting my bachelor's degree in marketing at Roosevelt University in Chicago, Illinois. The independent classes and nature of the curriculum gave me something to focus on in addition to my family. I would spend the next many years earning my Bachelor of General Studies degree in Business Institutions. At long last, in 1996, I received the letter saying "all requirements complete."

It was only natural Paul would want to have a party for me. As he was with all of my endeavors, Paul had been tremendously supportive, helping me with many a paper, encouraging me every step of the way. He was one of my greatest cheerleaders. While others might have been enchanted or maybe irritated with my idiotic ideas, he always championed them. I'm certain on some level he found them and me entertaining, rather than serious business propositions, though he was a smart man never to suggest I wouldn't succeed.

We loved parties, and from what I've been told, people loved to come to our parties. Good people, good food, good fun, good laughs…*all* the time! This party was no exception. Paul rented a bus, included 25 of my friends and family, and bought extra tickets to the commencement ceremony. Later, our house was full of family and friends, graduation gifts, food, wine, laughs. But in the midst of the celebrating, I had one of the most poignant moments of clarity.

As I had walked across the stage to receive my diploma, I couldn't even hear my friends cheering for me. Not even my children. I felt that it was very similar to how you must feel when you go to heaven. No matter how much you accumulate, how much you bring with you, in the end you must go by yourself. You can't take any of it with you. It would be a moment that I experienced by myself. When I shared that experience with a friend, she commented, "It is so interesting you had such vivid presence at that particular moment in time."

Eerily, I have come to recognize these moments of "energized presence" being in the company of others, yet very much alone. There are just some moments in time, some experiences one must experience alone. No matter how much we prepare, there will be times when we must leave our friends and family, our supporters, behind. We must trust in some fashion they will be there in spirit, but the situation, the experience must be managed as best we can with all we've got…ourselves.

Hugs and more hugs, Ken. Your friend, Cindy

BACK TO THE DESERT

Dear Ken,

In 1998, we moved to Phoenix. Visiting our winter home there over the years, Paul had grown to love Arizona as much as I did, and he also wanted to keep his promise that if I moved to Chicago for his career, he would, in some way, get us back to Phoenix. He kept his promise.

At the time I was promoting my ladies' financial groups and entertaining our many friends who wanted to come visit us in beautiful, sunny Arizona. Paul was looking for the next opportunity in his career.

The last couple of years had not been easy for Paul, work-wise. While he had been well rewarded financially, in truth, as President of Caremark Orthopedic Services Inc., he was strongly opposed to HealthSouth Corporation's acquisition of the 120 physical rehabilitation centers he had worked so hard to acquire in 13 states. His division was expecting revenues of nearly $80 million that year. While it was true at the time HealthSouth had revenues of $1.1 billion and operated nearly 600 outpatient and rehabilitation centers, Paul did not trust the founder, Richard Marin Scrushy. He felt strongly it wasn't a promising opportunity for the many employees of his division he so dearly cared about. He fought diligently with upper executives to discourage the acquisition. It was not to be. Paul refused to be a part of HealthSouth Corporation.

It would take a few years for Paul's instincts to prove correct. Richard Scrushy was convicted of 30 counts of money laundering, extortion, obstruction of justice, racketeering, and bribery (along with Alabama Governor Don Siegelman) in June 2006.

This is not a story I share to talk disparagingly of HealthSouth Corporation. My point is to share with you the heartfelt deep dedication and love Paul had for the many teams of professionals he worked with in the sports medicine world. You can now possibly understand why a move to Phoenix, a fresh start, would be good for him and for us. It was a time we both thought we could actualize our dream of spending the school year in Arizona and our summers in Montana, where we had purchased 21 acres of land with the severance Paul had received when he left Caremark.

We made the decision to put most of our things in storage and live in our much smaller winter home in Arizona. I rather enjoyed the quaintness of this desert lifestyle, but it didn't seem to bode well for Paul. He had challenges finding the right career opportunity. While he did find opportunities, truth be told, Phoenix, Arizona, is not a business or medical Mecca. I share these stories because I wonder if they were early warning signs of what would come to be big trouble for our marriage...and for Paul.

I remember thinking maybe it was living in our small winter home. Perhaps getting back into a home with more space would be the answer to the unrest. Paul had teamed up with his former partners and started another company in Seattle, and although he had only been involved with it for six weeks or so, it seemed we were back on the road to financial steadiness. I began working with a real estate agent to find our next property. We fell in love with our dream home on Carol Avenue in Scottsdale, and we bought it with the promise of a successful new business venture for Paul.

I remember the moment like it was yesterday. I was with the movers and my brother and sister, moving our things into our new home. Paul returned home from Seattle. I walked out the door in the garage, and as he passed me, he said, "I quit."

I responded, "You what?"

He simply repeated the same words: "I quit."

Oh dear God, how could this happen? Now we had a big house to maintain. It might take another long while before he would work again, but in hindsight, it was one of those hidden blessings in that Paul got to spend a great deal of time with our children and their activities. On the other hand, the time off work was not good for Paul. Too much idle time isn't good for anyone, especially Paul. He had a fondness for dive bars and unsavory people. They would be his downfall.

Trying to take the pressure off of Paul, I initiated many conversations about how to regroup, how to make things right again. I told him I would do whatever he wanted and needed to do to be happy in his career again. Should we consider Chicago, Connecticut, Los Angeles? Maybe move to Montana and live on our property? What could we do to make things right? Honestly, I don't think *he* even knew the answer to those questions. He favored being an entrepreneur; he did not want to go back into corporate America to work for someone else. What to do next?

Wives rarely know "exactly" what goes on in their husband's affairs, so while I don't know exactly what happened, it wasn't the first time Paul got irritated with the partners of a business relationship. Business investments we were personally funding, by the way. In truth, I was getting frustrated with the repeated conflicts in the business relationships, with Paul leaving the companies abruptly, and with considerable financial and professional damage.

There are always two, three, four sides to every story. But as far as my side went, I was tired of investing in businesses that weren't long-lasting and going well. So when Paul brought up the idea to get a second mortgage on our home to fund another business, I absolutely refused.

I was an odd duck in this time of American society. Everybody was getting second and sometimes third mortgages on their homes. It is a principle I have always maintained: real estate is an investment, not a bank. While prices might be escalating at a dizzying, intoxicating rate, this is the time to sell, not borrow money against the pretend dollars of supposed value.

Paul was very upset about my refusal, taking it as a personal affront to his business acumen. There is probably some truth to this. I had lost trust in him. Something was amiss. While I loved our home, I would not keep it at all costs. There was much to love about our home.

I loved each of our children's bedrooms. Each bedroom had its own bathroom and walk-in closet. I had decorated each room to match their particular tastes of the time. Doesn't every mother want her daughter to have a princess castle painted on her wall with pixie dust sprinkled on it to make it sparkle? A bedroom decorated in a baseball or animal theme for her sons?

Our master bedroom was huge, with cathedral ceilings, large walk-in closet, French doors to the pool and Jacuzzi, beautiful fireplace, oversized bathroom. A photo of Paul and me in jean jackets hung over our fireplace. Yet another custom photo over our dresser of me and my daughter Michelle. I wanted a photo to honor and remember my motherhood.

Every mother wants a family room full of photo albums archiving the family memories. Every mother wants the oversized photo of the family holding hands in Hawaii at the beach in the entry way, complete with white shirts and denim shorts, next to the grand piano. We used to joke when someone asked, "Who plays the piano?" We responded, "It plays itself!"

Of course, there was the 6-by-4-foot collage we kept at the front door, which we created together as a family about our family. It became a family habit to make suggestions of what to add to our collage. An Uno card, a Scrabble piece, napkins from restaurants, lyrics from favorite songs, ticket stubs from activities—it was fun to have the kids ask, "Mom, can we add this to the collage? Is this a good idea?"

A Woman of Interest

Our home was a place of peace and plenty. I had (and still have) a quote framed at the entrance to my home: "To all those who enter, may our home be a place of peace and plenty, strength and sanctuary, warmth and laughter. A place where love resides."

Those weren't just warm sentiments; it was really the way Paul and I liked to live. We entertained often. Whether it was one of our children's sports team parties, birthday parties, or family gatherings, we enjoyed having the gatherings at our home. Many a friend traveled from out of town when they needed refuge or just some good old-fashioned fun. Paul was quick to fire up the barbeque, prepare dinner, or make a pitcher of margaritas. We were known for our inclusive entertaining. I don't know that entertaining is even the correct word. We weren't really entertaining. Most people felt very comfortable in our home. There were enough rooms to spread out: seven bedrooms, seven bathrooms, and a basement. In Arizona, having a full basement was quite a big deal. This always amused me, as us Kansas girls were used to everyone having a basement. But for some reason, here in Arizona basements are few and far between. Our home was especially nice with every feature—from theatre room to tennis court, from batting cage and swimming pool to wine cellar, our home was a wonderful sanctuary.

Of course, it would have been heartbreaking to leave or have to change the family surroundings, and fortunately, by living off of our savings and investments, and by Paul consulting for a time, we managed to stay in our dream home and maintain our lifestyle. Using my marketing skills and fondness for entrepreneurship, I began to explore the Oprah mantra of the day: "Do what you love." I loved to give gifts, so I created CZ Custom Gift Design. I had been told many times that people enjoyed the unique gifts I created for them, which usually included some type of poetry or clever wording. I liked finding gifts for my friends and family, teachers, and business associates.

While Oprah's idea was a good one and I enjoyed CZ Custom Gift Design, in order to be a success at my business, it meant making one heck of a lot of gifts. While I enjoyed making gifts for those I cared about, I quickly found the exhausting physical work of making gifts for strangers not to be my passion.

I enjoyed the learning process of CZ Custom Gift Design. My friend Lynn Reilly traveled with me, working the booths at the gift mart in Atlanta, going to gift shows to display my creations (in particular the Wedding Expo here in Arizona), creating a website, and meeting my close friend Michael Blank at SCORE, an organization to help beginning entrepreneurs organize their business. A natural salesperson, I reached out to local businesses to buy my product.

At the same time, I continued to create more of our many family traditions, like that of our children and their caretakers getting a gift every day when Paul and I traveled; a tradition created so the kids would always feel secure we would return. Three more gifts, three more days until Mommy and Daddy would return. I wanted them to know they were loved and thought about while we traveled. We traveled often, Paul and I, and our family. We believed in spending our money on experiences rather than things. We loved first-class traveling.

In particular, Paul loved to travel to our property on the Yellowstone River in Montana. It was his heaven on Earth, his sanctuary, the place that centered him. We kept a large photo of the property above our fireplace. Once we were financially secure again, we planned to build a dream cabin on the river. Everyone who knew us knew this was Paul's dream.

In the meantime, while our property was without a house, we spent many summers at Mountain Sky Guest Ranch in Emigrant, Montana. It was truly paradise.

We made many friends each week we spent at the ranch. Our children could roam free, and there were plenty of activities, horseback riding, wonderful food, great fishing for Paul, a spa and a pool, and more friends for me.

I must admit these weeks at the dude ranch were not my favorite. I didn't particularly enjoy horseback riding or fishing,

A Woman of Interest

which were the main attractions. But I always had plenty of things to keep me busy: reading, writing, painting, letter and journal writing, and, of course, making new friends (my favorite).

I remember distinctly the year we met the Blank and Matney families. I had been in Eddie Matney's Phoenix-area restaurant earlier in the year talking with him about a CZ Custom Gift Design product. Eddie is a warm, gregarious, nationally respected chef. I remember so clearly knowing intuitively that it was beyond odd that our families would be in Montana, all the way from Arizona, for the same week.

Eddie and Paul became fast friends. They loved fly-fishing, loved their families, and enjoyed each other's company very much. Our families became very good friends. In the years to come, we would plan our weeks to the ranch to be the same so we could enjoy each other's company.

We have so many wonderful shared memories, but one in particular stands out, because it illustrates how Paul got along with everyone, wasn't intimidated by anyone, and had a great sense of humor. The ranch is known for great family activities. One week, Steven Spielberg and his family were at the ranch, too. As I recall, Saturday night was family skit night, and Paul and the kids were in the skit with Steven. I was video recording and taking photos of the fun. Paul, long known for his growling bark of a mad dog, did just that. I remember Steven laughing, saying to Paul, "That is the best bark I have ever heard! If I need one for a movie, I'm calling you!" It was a favorite family story.

In truth, though, by now we had begun to travel apart rather than together more frequently. We had enjoyed trips to the Winter and Summer Olympics, and were fortunate enough to see the Dream Team basketball players in Barcelona, and skied the French Alps in Albertville. Paul's physical therapy company was the sponsor for the athletes. We lived large. It was wonderful. I do not share this with you to impress you, Ken. I share it with you so that you can understand how dramatic the pending lifestyle adjustments required of our family were.

When no one is working to bring in an income, investments are being depleted, and the stock market is declining at an alarming rate, tough choices must be made. It is in these times of tough choices that couples, in my opinion, show the strength of their relationship, their alchemy, if you will. Our alchemy had always been exceptional. I told Paul he had the "Midas touch," and I believed it. He believed it, too. Everything he touched turned to gold. With our combination of skills, we were closer to platinum. We were good at assessing risks and opportunities, dividing responsibilities, and attaining goals. But something had happened.

Little did I know.

I must stop for now, Ken. I will write you more another day. Now it *must* be time for a glass of wine or a hike or lunch with a friend.

Hugs, your friend, Cindy

A Woman of Interest

THE UNRAVELING

Dear Ken,

It is understandable it would be difficult to give up. Like so many Americans, from 2005 to 2010, difficult decisions had to be made about homes and finances. We were no different. With our financial reserves, we had been able to enjoy a good life as Paul looked for his next business opportunity. The last one had not gone well. In June 2006 there was an "Employment Termination General Release Agreement" between Paul and his employer/company Upstream Rehabilitation. It was an agreement signed between him and David Van Name, his longtime business partner. They had been partners for many, many years. We both liked and respected Dave. It could not have been an easy contract to draw up or sign. In addition to Dave being Paul's business partner, he was one of Paul's closest friends. I consider him and his wife to be good friends to my family to this day.

Like so many Americans, our family was disheveled. We had made the mutual decision that Paul would be the main breadwinner. I was the stay-at-home Mom making traditional decisions. Unfortunately, it had been a time of reconciling our roles. Paul wasn't all that excited to work. I wasn't all that excited to stay at home. The kids were getting older. They didn't need as much of my time.

Around 2005, through my work with CZ Custom Gift Design, I became connected with Chuck Sorenson, then president of P.S. I Love You! Inc. (I sold his product line of cards through my company and spoke at his annual meeting.) This connection only added fuel to the fire of my passion to promote the handwritten note, and I decided to form a new company, Writing In Style—a resource for education, advocacy, and product offerings celebrating and preserving the handwritten word. I began to write a column for Pen World International magazine on the subject. (Yes, I refer to myself as "the self-appointed handwritten note advocate.")

Paul, for his part, was struggling with being unemployed, searching for that next golden business opportunity. He took to hanging out at the local bars with a new circle of friends. Those bars were, in large part, our downfall. I was very uncomfortable with the hours he spent and the people that he hung out with in these places. The consequences were getting bigger. I couldn't stand it. I was getting very frustrated, even embarrassed, by his accelerating aggressive behavior and the consequences. There were brushes with the law. The situation was making me more and more uncomfortable. Because of our lifestyle, traveling often with friends and family in many cities, I think we believed our troubles were hidden from most people. But I'm fairly certain we were wrong; most of our friends and family knew there was trouble in paradise.

It would take me ten years to finally realize I had to leave the man of my dreams, the father of my children. I had to leave the big, beautiful house, our dream home. I had to leave our lifestyle of international travel, romantic meals, interesting social circles, generous, thoughtful gifts, my best friend, my confidant. It was getting too dangerous to be married to Paul. Little did I know how dangerous it would be to divorce him.

Never in a million years, Ken, would people think our lives would end up as they did. To this day, people ask me, "Cindy, this doesn't make sense. Why were you divorcing someone that you say was a great father, a great husband, a great man?"

Again, it's that gut feeling, that intuition that something was terribly wrong. It will be one of the mysteries I am surely to ponder for a long time. I really don't know what happened to Paul. But he had changed. The behaviors of his last few years were so far out of his character. It was not an easy decision to divorce him. It wasn't a decision I made quickly.

I had been in counseling with Dr. David McPhee, a Phoenix-based psychologist who specializes in family forensic psychology. I adore him. You know by now, Ken, that I adore everyone in my life, Dr. McPhee included. While he was surprised on February 12, 2007, when I told him I had moved out of our home and into an apartment, he was well aware of the many challenges I had been facing in the last years of my marriage. Those stories, however, I will leave between me and my counselor.

After the initial shock and hearing my explanation as to what had prompted this decision, Dr. McPhee was very concerned about my legal position. He feared I would be characterized as abandoning my family in divorce proceedings. He wanted me to meet with a divorce attorney right away. It never crossed my mind to fear divorce proceedings or work with lawyers.

To my way of thinking, there are laws that protect us. Lawyers are there to educate us and represent us to navigate the court system. I had no idea how the legal system worked. I had no idea I would be accused of a lot worse than just abandoning my family. That's not how all lawyers operate, I was to learn.

I followed Dr. McPhee's advice and interviewed the three attorneys he suggested. I was particularly drawn to the collaborative divorce. Collaborative divorce was the newest method of alternative dispute resolution in family law at the time, and was described as employing cooperative techniques rather than adversarial strategies and litigation. It is highly suggested when there is little disagreement and there are children involved.

As Paul and I both had prior divorces that were amicable, I assumed our divorce would be the same. With a 23-year marriage, in a community property state, Paul and I were generally able to agree about the parenting of our children and our financial decisions. It seemed reasonable to me we would be able to have a collaborative divorce. Paul agreed to consider this and meet with the collaborative divorce attorney.

I thought we would have a friendly divorce. One of the reasons I felt secure in marrying Paul was the way in which he spoke of his first wife; the way he handled their divorce. The way, frankly, he spoke of all women. He was a fair, generous man. We respected each other as parents, fellow human beings. I trusted him. We just couldn't be married any longer. How could it not go well?

We went to the appointment. Given the nature of the questions, comments, and our interactions with the collaborative attorney, I was 95% sure that Paul would agree to a collaborative divorce. He didn't. He told me the next day, after having thought it over, that he wanted us to get separate attorneys. He wanted a traditional divorce. His decisions were so unpredictable. In retrospect, I wonder if others goaded him into this decision.

I met my divorce attorney on March 5, 2007. "Meeting with client to retain. One hour at $300.00 an hour. Total Charge $300.00." That's how my relationship with Steve R. Smith of Fromm, Smith, Gadow, P.C., began. He seemed a good man, a gentleman; he represented me in a pleasant, fair manner. I followed Steve's directions. That's what made sense to me. If I ask for advice, especially if I'm paying for it, I should listen to it. Steve always seemed of sound mind, though I must admit, he surprised me time after time as the divorce proceedings would unfold.

Proceedings began with me providing answers to five questions in a family court cover sheet:

1. Is anyone mentioned on this cover sheet currently a victim of any family or domestic violence?

2. Has anyone listed on this cover sheet been the plaintiff, defendant, or named in a petition for an Order of Protection?

3. Was the order of protection granted by the Maricopa County of Superior Court?

4. Are any of the children named above in any physical danger due to abuse or neglect?

5. Has anyone named on this sheet had any involvement with Child Protective Services in Arizona?

I answered "no" to all five questions. I was wrong. My children were in grave danger, as was Paul. Or perhaps I just repressed signals that were too frightening to deal with.

Our three children were 18, 15, and 12 at the time. Paul had been a great father. One of the best I know. To the best of my knowledge at the time, there was no reason for Paul and me not to share joint custody of our three wonderful children. One week in his home. One week in my home. We would work together to finish raising our children; children we both loved and treasured very much.

The first court orders started arrived with wording like, "Don't harass, don't bother, don't physically abuse, don't take children out of the state, don't hide earnings, don't take out a loan, don't sell community property, don't discontinue health insurance," on and on. The "rules" couldn't have set well with Paul, and the wording surprised me. When I asked, my attorney about it, Steve assured me it was standard wording, nothing to be concerned about. He didn't know Paul.

Paul was a proud man, a *very* proud man. Failure, changing courses, or accepting that courses needed to change were not his strengths. There are few that could disagree with this. He was proud of his career, his home, his family. He hated being told what to do.

We had been told not to sell community property by the courts. In the divorce proceedings, the first time I began to think I might be in trouble was when a real estate agent (who was a friend of mine) called from Montana, telling me our 21 acres on the Yellowstone River in Livingston was up for sale. What was Paul doing? This single act was so much more telling than selling community property.

But the real estate agent didn't want to know what he was doing. She wanted to ask me, "Did I know the property was for sale? Did I know there was a full price, cash offer? Did I know if we were accepting the offer? Paul wouldn't respond to the deal." So it began, creating chaos or chaos being created because of actions and then no response.

I reached out to my divorce attorney for advice on one chaotic situation after another. It wasn't just me who saw the change in Paul. Anyone who communicated with him during the last years of his life could see the change. The challenge was that he made it very difficult to communicate or to reason with him.

Intuition, gut feeling. When you've been married to someone for more than 20 years, actions become somewhat predictable. In his final years, Paul's were far from his normal behavior. A driven, successful man, being out of work for two years was taking its toll, not only on our finances, but also on his self-esteem. And while pride or strong self-confidence can be a great strength, at the other end of the spectrum it can be known as hubris.

I did not know of this word "hubris" until a friend introduced it to me. Barb and her husband were close personal and professional friends. They knew us well—so well, that when she explained hubris to me, it frightened me. She was trying to give me a wake-up call. She said, "Cindy, this is hubris. By definition, the actions of over-confident pride and arrogance, with a lack of humility generally combined with fame and money that results in a violent death. It is also referred to as 'pride that blinds,' causing one to act in foolish ways that belay common sense."

It was this ongoing lack of common sense that my divorce attorney and I tried to negotiate with, a man known for doing things his own way. This wasn't all that out of character. But he usually made decisions that were in the best interest of his family, his friends, his colleagues. Those weren't necessarily his ways in the last years of his life.

It didn't take a genius to realize quickly that this divorce wasn't going to go well. Paul did not like being told what to do, nor did I.

It was the year 2007. The real estate market, particularly in Arizona, was tumbling. The stock market was dropping. Our personal assets had been hit hard. We weren't broke, but we couldn't afford to be careless. It was time for both Paul and me to go back to work. It was time to cut back on expenses. These were sentiments I had been chanting for a long while. Paul and I weren't on the same page. We weren't even in the same chapter.

As we began the painful process of dividing our assets, it became clear we would need to sell our beautiful home, our dream home. I reached out once again to our real estate agent, Wendy Cyr, who was a friend. She knew how terribly difficult this decision was for our family. She knew us well. Wendy, too, experienced the startling differences in the new Paul.

Wendy had been part of the excitement of us buying our first winter home in Arizona, and she navigated the purchase and sale of our dream home. She helped both Paul and me find our post-divorce properties. She helped the estate sell Paul's house after his death. Yes, she knew us well.

I struggle to find the words to describe the professionalism, the dedication, the compassion Wendy has shown my family. Keep in mind that with the poor real estate market of that time in Arizona and a tumultuous divorce, she had her work cut out for her. There was opportunity in the collapsed real estate market. There always is. But a person needs to be diligent in their decisions and their research, and after that a portion of luck is probably needed as well.

Frankly, I'm surprised she didn't walk away from us. There's not enough money in the world to earn from all of the chaos we caused her. Truth be told, she cared and still cares about our family.

There are two moments of friendship I remember so clearly with Wendy. One, in the midst of utter chaos, we were standing in the parking lot of the apartment complex into which I had moved. She knew how terribly upset I was about the divorce, my family, and the details of selling our home. I remember her taking my hands and saying, "I care." Two simple words: "I care." Honestly, I don't think Wendy knew how my family was going to survive, but she stuck with us, and for that I am very, very grateful.

The second memory was when we finally sold our home. It wasn't easy, but Wendy got the job done. Paul was very upset about the sale, but he would need to sign the papers to close the deal. Wendy couldn't get him to respond to e-mail or phone messages. She needed to go to our home to get his signature. We decided to go together. We were both nervous with what might be going on.

As I recall, we walked to the garage, I waited on the periphery, as I was no longer permitted in our home because of the divorce. Wendy entered the house yelling out Paul's name. Finally, he slowly came walking down the long hallway. He resigned himself to signing the papers. He looked at Wendy and asked, "What am I supposed to do now?" She replied, "You need to move, Paul."

Wendy and I were both grateful we found Paul safe and sound that day. It scared us both very much. Wendy would indeed help both Paul and me find our next homes. Wendy Cyr is not only one of the best real estate agents in Phoenix, but she is one of my dearest friends.

By May 2007, the notion of a friendly divorce would be long gone. The division of assets wouldn't be easy. The co-parenting of our children wouldn't be easy. Nothing was going to be easy. Surely it was my entire fault, this ugly divorce, and I was making Paul crazy with my demands for spousal maintenance, child support, trying to take the children from him. No matter what information my attorney provided the courts, no matter the expert after expert hired to show concern for my children and Paul, in the end, the courts, the judges, and Paul's family would not believe that Paul was in trouble, serious trouble.

Especially when I was the mother who left the family home, left this great guy. I *must* have been exaggerating the facts at hand—especially when fabricated stories began to be circulated about my

A Woman of Interest

habitual lying, psychotic disorders, promiscuity, drunken stupors, and drug-seeking trips to Mexico.

It was said that I was jealous of Paul, his happiness, and his new friends from the bar. My children told me that Dad liked to play pool at the bar and that there was nothing wrong with it. But in truth, our children were very concerned about Paul, too.

Do I sound bitter, Ken? I'm really not. I was stunned. I've come to live comfortably with all types of untruths being said about me. After so many years of character assassination, I've come to live in peace with it. Besides, at the time I followed my attorney Steve's advice each step of the way: "Tell the truth, it will set you free."

Interesting. It seemed my truths would be used against me time and time again. Slowly but surely my life would be ripped to shreds. Like an infectious disease, it began so slowly that when I finally accepted the harsh truths from family, friends, or professionals, I had already gotten myself in some very precarious situations. Without the keen wisdom and courage of my friends, family, and highly trained professionals, who knows where I would be today.

Paul no longer was the man I knew or loved. He had made a new circle of friends and couldn't be convinced they might not be the best people for him to hang around. I had followed my divorce attorney's advice, my counselor's advice. We had presented mounds of information to the courts trying to describe the trouble Paul was in, the danger my children were in.

It would not be enough to convince Paul or the courts that danger was lurking. When my divorce attorney said to me, "Cindy, you must hire a private investigator to prove what he is doing. Right now, it's your word against his."

A private investigator? I'm supposed to hire a private investigator to follow the father of my children? I was dumbfounded. I didn't even know where one finds a private investigator. Fortunately for me, I had a friend who knew one well. The investigator's name was Jon M. Craig. I remember meeting him for the first time in a restaurant. He seemed like a nice, matter-of-fact kind of guy. He assured me he had done this many times. He assured me—promised me—that he would treat Paul with respect.

I was mortified of the task at hand. I paid Jon the fees and left to attend a Stationery Show meeting in New York City. I was grateful to be out of town when the surveillance would take place.

I remember telling my sister about the developments. Her response: "Cindy, it will be the easiest money the detective ever earns."

"Why?" I asked.

She said, "He goes to the same bar every day, at the same time. He walks by my hair salon." She [the stylist] had been upset for me because she was a family friend. She had known of our family's painful divorce. She knew and saw each day the shell of a man Paul used to be, walking to the same bar every day, between 10:30 and 11 in the morning.

My sister was right, as she usually is. It was a very strange, out-of-body, out-of-mind experience, at least for me, to have a private investigator involved. I remember there being part of me that wanted to have the evidence to show Paul was out of sorts. And another part wanted me to be terribly wrong. I wanted to believe he was looking for gainful employment, but was unable to find anything to suggest it.

The first night of the surveillance I spent with a close friend in New York City. We locked the door to our hotel room and drank martinis. As he would remind me, "There is not enough alcohol in the world to block out the task at hand." We gave it a good shot. I so wanted to block out the world and my troubles, if only for one night.

We waited for the investigative reports. I was heartbroken. Paul was indeed in the bars of our neighborhood each day, all day. He did indeed have a new circle of friends who were very different from our past circle of friends. The video surveillance would have to be given to opposing counsel.

I had hoped this would be the wake-up call that would bring Paul to his senses. It was not. It just added fuel to the fire of the long divorce proceedings.

A Woman of Interest

Paul shared with our kids that I had had him followed. They were upset with me. He was upset with me. I wasn't a popular person in my family. And to be certain, I understood how he felt about it. The next day, after learning of the surveillance, Paul began to park his car in a very obvious front parking space at the bar. The message was very clear: "Fuck you. I will do what I want."

After mounds of evidence, it was the court's decision that it was safe for our children to spend 50 percent of their time with their father. Their father was of sound mind. How could the courts make such a decision? I was devastated, my family and friends were devastated. How could they miss it, with all of the evidence we had provided? They wouldn't miss it the next time. We would be on television, in the newspapers, in the police blotters.

I wanted to move as far away as I could, and in fact, had been waiting to buy a special casita I had found and fallen in love with. My divorce attorney had told me it might not set right with the courts if I moved just this short 20 minutes away. So, I waited.

When the court rulings were handed down, I could then decide on my future home. It didn't really make any difference where I lived; the kids would be spending half of their time in each of our homes.

I couldn't get away fast enough. It is embarrassing to have your ex-husband self destruct in the same town where once we were involved in so many family, community circles. Further, it's tiring to be the one ringing the bells of alarm. After a while, it wears everyone out. I was worn out.

I would move to my casita, I would begin my new life. I would create a safe haven for my kids. I understood the rulings. I would make the best of them.

That seems to be what I do best, make the best of things. The best of *these* things would last a short period of time; things were going to change again in six months.

I love my casita. I love my community; I love Casa Blanca, Paradise Valley, Arizona. Casa Blanca is a very special, unique treasure of a community. There are 113 distinct homes, set in 19 acres of exotic grounds. It's known for upwardly mobile, affluent empty-nesters and second homeowners.

With a rose garden, a cactus garden, three pools, tennis courts, and beautiful grounds to walk through, I thought I had found heaven on Earth when I first entered. My casita is one of the larger casitas, with four rooms that could be used as bedrooms or dens.

I thought I had found the perfect place, as I wasn't certain how many children I would have living with me. But I wanted them to all know there was plenty of room for them and I wanted them to be a part of my life. I thought the amenities would somehow replace those we had left behind in our big home. I liked the close proximity to restaurants, shopping, nightlife, the airport, and downtown. I liked my neighbors, soon to be friends. In fact, in the first days, I would walk the grounds in the evenings to ward off the hours and days of not having my family with me when they were in Paul's care—one week on, one week off, that was our custody agreement. And of course I loved how close my casita was to Camelback Mountain and hiking. These things would serve to save my sanity. If there was indeed any left.

Of all the things I couldn't face, it was the deterioration of my children's lives. Just one thing after another, and there was nothing I could do. One of my children didn't want to see me; in fact, hadn't seen me in a year. A child I loved and still love dearly. Another child was well on his way to adulthood, so it seemed. And my baby girl (a "baby" in my mind, although she was 13) was ill. She was excited to go to camp for four weeks. Who could blame her? A month away from the craziness? *I* wanted to go to camp.

She was diagnosed with shingles. Our family pediatrician, Arturo Gonzales, one of the most respected pediatricians in the Valley and long devoted to our family and to the children through the tumultuous divorce, told me, "Cindy, I can't approve her to go to camp with shingles. She must be clear of them before I can sign the release." He knew how upset we both were with this news, but

A Woman of Interest

she needed rest and relief from the pain. I had just a few days to get her healthy. We were under the wire, because it usually took much longer. But I promised her I would do everything in my power to get her healthy. Mom would take care of it. Trust me.

Even this did not bring Paul to his senses, which is how I knew he was so very much out of sorts. In his right mind he would have never left his daughter in pain, in his home without air conditioning, to find her own way. She was just 13 years old.

When I learned she was laying on the tile floor to keep cool because the air conditioning was broken in his house, and that she had asked one of my son's friends to get her pain prescription filled, I calmly, respectfully, asked Paul, "Even though it's not my week, please may I come get Michelle and take care of her?" He agreed. Yes, I could take care of her.

My divorce attorney also told me, "Cindy, you have to give up the handwritten note and Writing In Style. You need to get a job, go back to work." I was heartbroken. I didn't mind the "getting a job" part. What I minded was that, after all my efforts, my passions and my business seemed to be gaining momentum, and I would have to focus on something else. I would have to give up writing my column for Pen World International magazine and the public speaking about the handwritten note.

I took his advice, as always, and got a job at the wonderful Hospice of the Valley in Phoenix. I loved my job there. I was grateful for it. From the beginning, I tried to keep my personal and professional life separate. It was not to be. In my background check, my Social Security number got mixed up, so the divorce needed to be discussed with my immediate supervisor. Other than that, I did not discuss my divorce with many of my professional associates.

In July 2008, I did not attend a 2:30 p.m. meeting. It's as simple as that. I had been at a company meeting at 10:30 in the morning. I had confirmed I would attend the 2:30 meeting. I didn't make it. I simply forgot. I was exhausted. My employer was worried about me. It was unlike me, it didn't seem reasonable. Something must have happened to me. When I finally checked my phone and saw the numerous calls looking for me, it was no surprise my manager was upset. Very upset.

I was called on the carpet, rightfully so. Did I understand people were looking for me? I disrupted the entire meeting. Yes, I understood. I apologized. I owned it. But it was a huge error. Tearfully, I explained to her that I had been sleeping, somewhat sleeping on the tile floor of my daughter's room for many nights trying to nurse her back to health so she could go to camp. I woke at her every movement, if I was ever asleep. I tried to keep her comfortable and allow her sweet little body to heal. I was exhausted. I simply forgot the 2:30 meeting.

Thankfully, my manager did not fire me. Though it was not a positive note in my employment record, if a note was indeed made, it would, however, be a mental note many would not forget for a long time.

But for some reason, I was able to keep on keeping on. Some believe this spirit, my spirit, which can't be brought down, is what motivates others to keep trying to bring me down. I don't know. I don't care. I know why and how I kept going: friends, family, gratitude, laughter, hiking, and enough wine to take the edge off. And that's the truth!

For some reason, I don't know why I was and am always able to find something or someone to be grateful for, someone to share a laugh with—and many times it simply can be me, myself, and I. That's fine with me, too. Honestly, the absurdity of my life is rather funny. Don't you think? After all, my glass is *always* half full.

Except for one night. I must be honest with you, Ken. There was one night I couldn't bear the chaos anymore. I couldn't find anything to laugh about. I was heartbroken, body broken, everything broken. The courts and the judges had made their final decisions. The assets had been divided. Paul and I were officially divorced; we were just waiting for the judge to sign the final documents.

A Woman of Interest

I was increasingly worried I was going to lose my job. My kids were faltering. Paul was out of control. I didn't see any way for all of this to end. I just couldn't take it anymore.

I share this story with the full understanding that there are those in our society who will judge me harshly as suicide has a very ugly intonation, maybe rightfully so. I'm used to all types of judgments by now. Who's to say? But in my mind, this was the deepest of my desperation and in honesty I must share it with you. Because, truly, I understand what it feels like to begin to believe there is no hope, no bright future. Similar to a sprig of rosemary, it is my hope you will always be able to remember a friendship in your moments of darkness. If you can't, call me. I will be your friend.

It was a summer night. I'd had my share of wine. To my way of thinking that night, my children were all secure. My daughter had gotten healthy enough to go to camp. My sons were in safe places. I decided to end my life.

I took close to 20 Ambien, a sleeping pill I had been pre-scribed. I think it's safe to say that was more than a mere plea for attention. Quite simply, I couldn't live one more moment of the craziness. I couldn't bear to watch one more atrocity happen to my children, myself, or to Paul.

Can you believe it? I couldn't even fucking commit suicide right. I woke up the next morning, with a terrible hangover and strange side effects, but alive nonetheless. It seemed nothing was ever going to be right again. How right I was about that. I would just get a couple of days to recover—the real madness was about to begin.

Let me go refill my cappuccino. I cannot think any more about this ugliness.

Hugs, your friend, Cindy

FACING THE UNFATHOMABLE

Dear Ken,

You've asked me to tell you about the murder. And you see how I avoid the topic? I will repeat some stories to you, want to tell you about my casita or friends, or heaven knows what, because I don't like talking or thinking about "it."

Ironically, during one of my pregnancies, the O. J. Simpson trial was on every network. I watched it every single day, every single hour. Paul and I would discuss it in the evenings. Actually, *I* would discuss it. He would listen for the most part. He did not like sensational television; neither did I. It was just all that was on television at the time. I got sucked into the day-to-day trial. I remember where I was when the verdict came in, on a way to a friend's house. I pulled over to watch the verdict announced in a restaurant. Like the rest of the world, I couldn't believe it. Little did I know that a similar nightmare would be coming *my* way. A woman who can't stand violence, who never allowed her kids to play with guns or watch violent movies. To think that such ugliness and violence could infiltrate our family is beyond unbelievable.

No longer am I writing about the romantic times of 1986, when Paul and I got married. I am writing about different moments in time; some days, possibly some weeks that were so heinous it is a staggering task. Most of what I write will come from the police investigation, my time with the police, and my gut instincts of spending 24 years in a very intimate relationship with Paul

Zimmermann. And then there is Tommy Sullivan. This guy had met my children, Paul's children. And yet, he could still kill their father? I will quite possibly never grasp this.

Someone comfortingly said to me once, "Cindy, they were drinking a lot."

Drinking a lot? Geez, *I* drink a lot. How much do you have to drink to plan to murder someone? And not ever come to the decision, that maybe, just maybe, it is a terrible thing to do. And even having never met me or known anything about me, he would use what I love most to organize his kill: pen and paper.

On one side of town I'm speaking publicly, privately, to anyone who will listen, about my passion: the values of a handwritten note. And on the other side of town, a madman is handwriting the bizarre "Tomasio Game Plan," outlining the details of his heinous crime that would devastate so many people. Paul had indeed changed.

It is documented that Paul spent his last day on earth with his new friends in their usual watering holes. It is documented that he left 92nd Street Café late afternoon/early evening on Thursday, July 10, 2008.

Ironically, our neighbors owned the restaurant/bar. I considered Chris a girlfriend, as we had spent many years together in a neighborhood book club and various other neighborhood social events. I basically considered her husband to be the husband of a girlfriend, but certainly a friendly neighbor, as we had also attended neighborhood social events. It was only natural that I called him when looking for Paul. But I'm getting ahead of myself.

It is documented that Paul Zimmermann and Tommy Sullivan went to Tommy Sullivan's house after a day of socializing. Paul went on his own accord, drove his own truck. Tommy did what he had been planning to do for some time. He shot Paul in the abdomen.

According to reports, there was excessive blood, and Paul did not die immediately. Without question, Paul would have struggled. Never in a million years would he have gone down without a fight. To fathom that this Georgetown Scholarship Football player could not win the most important fight of his life is unimaginable. Paul must have been very, very debilitated.

He would have fought, though he was against a foe that was driven with madness. How else can someone plot to kill another human being? A person who has had days upon days to reconsider his plan of murder? A person who has crossed paths with his children and friends? People that he knew would have their lives changed forever by his acts of greed and violence.

Sit and share beer after beer with the man he is planning on murdering? How does someone do that? In fact, he had moments to consider either phoning for help once Paul was shot or reaching for the rope to strangle him. Of course, madness chose the rope. I mean, after all, it was on his handwritten list of items titled, "Things I Need to Kill Paul Zimmermann."

Yes, the police found such a piece of paper in his home, lots of papers with lots of handwriting. Pages and pages of Tommy practicing forging Paul's signature and listing the LLCs he had created and used to steal Paul's money. Quite a number of them— eight accounts, as I recall—into which he transferred funds from Paul's accounts. Our financial statements were among Tommy's belongings, as was Paul's computer.

He had taken all of this from Paul's house. Paul had never noticed anything missing, because surely he would have taken exception to such an invasion. Paul wasn't great at keeping track of his money, he was known for his generosity. In our life together, it had become my responsibility to keep track of our finances and investments. I digress.

Also among Tommy's belongings were the things he did indeed acquire to kill Paul Zimmermann, per his handwritten list: gun, bullets, rope, tarp, gasoline. He was going to shoot him, strangle him, drag his body to a vacant lot, and burn his corpse beyond recognition. What had Paul ever done to him to earn such degrading disrespect for his life? His money? His dignity? Neither I nor anyone else will ever know the answers to those questions.

And to spend much energy thinking about it is really a waste of time. When such a traumatic tragedy happens to your family, time becomes even more important. What one does and has done with one's time becomes of paramount importance. There will be a lot to do, to navigate, in the aftermath of a senseless crime.

Few people think of this as the nightly news, the daily paper, the rampant violence in movies and games entertain them. For when the cameras are turned off, it is the family and friends of the loved one who sit in the ashes of destruction and wonder how they will ever rebuild their lives.

In my family's case, *literally* the ashes. Paul's human body was said to be one of the worst decomposed bodies the Scottsdale police had ever had to identify. Although for some reason the murderer did not use the gasoline to burn Paul's body as he had planned, he did dump his body in a vacant lot. The blazing Arizona July heat would accomplish the final annihilation of Paul's remains. It would take the investigators a while to positively, without a doubt, identify Paul, once he was found.

When a family member goes missing, there is always an uneasy gut-wrenching fear that something terribly wrong has happened. I did, indeed, still love and care about Paul; I just couldn't be married to him anymore. I wanted him to have a loving, fulfilling life. This was not to be.

It was completely within the frame of imagination that Paul would befriend these new guys he met in the typical suburban sports bars. They liked to play pool, drink beer, and watch sports, starting early in the day and going long into the evening. These were the kind of guys he liked.

He wasn't much for chasing the girls or expensive gambling. He dabbled in gambling a little here and there, but don't get me wrong, although he loved to play cards, poker, and craps, he didn't do it for the money. He did it for the sport. He loved a good game. Most importantly, he loved to win, *had* to win.

Paul had great pride in his one-arm pushups, pride in being the toughest guy in the room. He had to be the best. And that would be the attraction to this group of guys. He could be the best while his career was in a stage of uncertainty.

So, the police tell me, he struggled, he got strangled, and he died. And this is where Paul's part in the story ends, at least in Earthly form. He no doubt has moved into a different form. I feel him around me all the time. I know that he guides me. Not in language, but in a sixth sense. I know this with every fiber of my being. I also know with every fiber of my being he will not rest until he has put the pieces of our lives, our family, back together.

Anyone who does not believe this did not know Paul. He is sick with himself for allowing this to happen to our family, because his family—his three children—were the most important things in his life.

As far as Tommy goes, killing someone—not just anyone, but the father of my children, my husband for 23 years—wasn't the end of his deed. He needed to get rid of the body. I can only give you the facts, because I can't even begin to comprehend or understand the following details:

Tommy somehow got Paul's lifeless body behind the washing machine in his garage.

After a day or so, Tommy's live-in girlfriend noticed an "odor" in the garage. When asked about it, Tommy explained to her that a bird had died there.

When Tommy learned there was an ongoing police investigation, he decided to move Paul's body.

He wrapped Paul's body in a tarp, tied it to the back of his truck, and dragged it down the street to dump at the construction site of a new housing development.

Neighbors saw him dragging the bundled, stuffed blue tarp down the street, leaving a trail of some type of moisture. They assumed it was lawn scraps he was taking to the dump. The moisture was Paul's body fluids. The bundle was Paul's body.

He left Paul's body behind, got back in his truck, and drove away.

In the meantime, local friends and family, including myself, were searching everywhere for Paul. The local media and the police detectives were doing their best to find our missing family member. The police assigned our family a police advocate. I never knew such a position existed.

Police advocate, description of nature of work: provides on-scene contact with victims of violent crime and other trauma, crisis intervention, individual and family support, information about the criminal justice system, support agency referrals, aides in acquiring emergency shelter and facilitation of other immediate needs of victims.

Our police advocate was Natalie Summit. I worship the ground she walks on and could never repay her for all of the kindness and good counsel she gave my family and me. To say I am eternally grateful is the understatement of my lifetime.

To stay in sequence of events so as not to confuse you, I will share with you facts I know from the police investigation. Paul died on Thursday, July 10, 2008. On Friday morning, the very next day, Tommy drove by Paul's house, crossing paths with my son Kevin as he pulled out of the driveway of Paul's home. They did not speak, only exchanged glances.

Friday and Saturday Kevin and Paul's friends looked for Paul. On Sunday, the police were notified.

Tommy was waiting for, probably expecting, the police who knocked on his front door on July 14, 2008. The police asked him if he was Tommy Sullivan. He replied, "No." They asked him for identification. He closed the door to his home, went back into his house, and shot and killed himself.

The article in the Thursday, July 17, 2008, issue of the Arizona Republic read: "As part of a bizarre murder-suicide case, Paul Zimmermann, 48…on July 14, the investigation led police to the home of Tom Sullivan, 55, in the 9300 block of East Dreyfus Place. When police asked Sullivan for identification, he disappeared into the home, then shot and killed himself. Police followed drag marks at Sullivan's house to a vacant lot where they found Zimmerman's body."

Once you are in this ugly world of public violence, murder, and traumatic tragedy, it is very difficult, if not impossible, to get out of it. No matter how far one goes, physically or emotionally, to have a close intimate relationship with others, the question inevitably comes up, "What happened to the father of your children?"

I guess this must be the reason I write. He was a wonderful father, a devoted husband, and dedicated career man. He adored his mother and his father. He had a loving extended family of sisters, brothers, brother-in-laws, sister-in-laws, nieces, and nephews.

He was respected nationally as a champion for quality healthcare. Many cherished him as a friend. He did not deserve this tragic ending to his life. But then who really does?

I must change perspectives now. I must go back in time because there is a bit more to this story. Although one friend said to me, "Cindy, this did not happen to *you*, it happened to Paul," one cannot be around such violence and not be impacted by the explosion.

It simply never crossed my mind that I would be considered a suspect in Paul's disappearance or death. While I was busy looking for him, caring for my children, it just never crossed my mind to think of anything else but finding Paul.

Once we knew of his death, the immediate need was caring for the tremendous shock and pain of my children. My grieving was a bit different from everyone else's. Mine had been going on for many years, and in fact, evidence had been showing up throughout our divorce that Paul wasn't the man I married.

I missed him, although I knew I had to let him go. I had tried everything in my power and imagination to bring back the Paul I loved. He didn't seem to want to come back. He had chosen a path and no one could convince him it might not be a good one.

Now there are dead bodies. And there is no going back, ever. There were so many questions, questions that had to be answered.

Who was a part or knew about Tommy's plan? Speculation began. Word spread through the TV news, the papers, the gossip mills, and the pillow talk: maybe, just maybe, Paul's wife could be part of such a heinous crime.

How do friends, family, acquaintances, strangers react? And when I say "react," I don't mean not only with the power of their words, I mean with the power of their actions. Their actions surprised and stunned. Actually, that's an understatement. Everything is an understatement. *Everything* is so far over the top. I could not even begin to comprehend the surprises that were going to be coming my way. The stakes were very high, higher than I could ever imagine.

Trust me, the police don't get into all of this "touchy feely" stuff like I do. They want the facts. They have a crime to solve, for surely there will be another crime. There will be public outcry if we are not all reassured that the bad guys, the criminals, are off the streets. We all want to go back into our homes, turn off the lights, and sleep peacefully.

It is normal to be thankful that the tragedy did not strike our family. Thank God, thank the universe, thank whatever, whomever one believes in. It didn't happen to us. It happened to another family.

But this time it *did* happen to my family. And the craziness got even crazier. There were questions about me being part of Tommy Sullivan's murderous scheme. Now, let's stop for a minute. I'd like for you, Ken, to really think about what it could possibly feel like to have such a falsehood being thought about you.

No, please think about it a bit more.

It is beyond unfathomable to me that this was a thought or even a consideration. I guess it is reasonable, in hindsight, for the police to consider it. Though at the time, it didn't cross my mind, even as a soon to be ex-wife, that I would be a suspect. But for those who knew me, really knew me, how could they think such a thing?

I can hardly grapple with the reality that this horrific crime even happened to Paul or honestly happens to any human being.

I don't like violence, don't like to watch it, don't like to talk of it. But for those trying to rationalize or find peace, there has to be an answer. There has to be a reason for such nastiness.

And for some, I guess I was the answer. I was responsible for this terrible nightmare. I must not be too dramatic here. The fact of the matter is, there were, or might still be, just a few, possibly no more than a handful of people who ever seriously thought I was involved. A couple of years later, I met John C. Little, Jr. who was the city manager of Scottsdale at that time, and we became friends. He knew who I was, although I had no idea who he was or how he knew of me. He confirmed that I had been a "person of interest" with the detectives for a short period of time.

At the end of the day, their opinion is really the only one that mattered, for they would be determining my fate. I would like to think it was my stellar performance down at the police station, but who knows.

Is it too soon for humor? Can we begin to laugh again? Can we move on from the details of this horrendous crime to talk of the wonderful, generous acts of friendship and love I experienced? Because you know, Ken, that is really what I want to write about. I want to tell you about those acts of friendship in the darkest of moments that carried me through. That is why I love my thank-you card, created by Tara Dixon. It is from her stationery line called Gratitude Designs. She created the brand of my company, Writing In Style: a rosemary sprig, which symbolizes the remembrance of friendship, evolving from the dark shadows of thank you after thank you after thank you. *That* is the story. Not the story of nastiness, death, and tragedy. The story is about friendship and kindness.

Thank God I was unsuccessful at my earlier suicide attempt. My kids would not have had a parent had I succeeded in killing myself. The murderer was well on his path. He would have had no way of knowing I was dead, and clearly he would have cared less. What a strange turn of events.

I share with you one of my favorite sayings from the Talmud: "Every blade of grass has its angel that bends over it and whispers grow, grow." And don't I know it. I have more angels than any human deserves—also more friends, more family, and more blessings.

From this day forward, in any moments of doubt, I always reflect on these five blessings:

1. My three children were spared by Tommy Sullivan. For this I am eternally grateful.

2. No matter what our future holds, no matter what anyone says, I am grateful for the many years and memories I have had with my three children. No one will ever be able to take those away from me or distort them in my heart. If not one more memory is ever created I am grateful for our family memories.

3. My family's future is brighter than I can ever imagine. There are those that might try to undermine us, but that is their business and not mine. I know for certain with every fiber of my being that Paul is in heaven guiding us. He will not rest peacefully until our family is complete in love and peace.

4. There are those who always have it worse. Always.

5. I am eternally grateful for the kindness and support of my family and friends. I don't know how I will ever repay them.

I thought one chapter had closed. I was beginning my new life, a new chapter. My divorce settlement was finally completed. It was definitely a new chapter, but it certainly wasn't the chapter I had expected.

My divorce attorney was vacationing in California with his family when all this drama unfolded. I called his cell phone. I took him by surprise. While my divorce attorney and I had an amiable relationship, calls to his cell phone were far and few between, and certainly not when he was on vacation.

My first question was simple, "Steve, do you know if the divorce papers have been signed?" No, he did not. After sharing the tragic news of Paul's death, I will never forget his response, "Cindy, we knew something bad was going to happen, but we never thought it would be this bad. I am so sorry for your loss." Yes, he would check with the court to see if the judge had signed the divorce papers.

That one handwritten signature would decide whether I was married, widowed, or single.

I was divorced. Somewhere in the business hours of July 10, 2008, the judge had signed our divorce papers. Paul died later that evening. I was divorced by less than three hours. My divorce papers were signed the same day Paul died.

Little did I know, I was far from divorced. I was just beginning another divorce. Mark, my brother-in-law—ex-brother-in-law—would do his own version of divorcing me. While I had divorce papers, legal binding documents, they were barely worth the paper they were written on, the thousands of dollars spent on legal fees, or the months of agony. Mark would see to that.

There seems to be a pattern here, isn't there? I seem to surprise people often. Have I surprised you yet, Ken?

Is it an acceptable time for a glass of wine, or perhaps a bottle of wine? Maybe it's time for my daily hike. There is always a friend available to listen, to hold me, to shake his or her head at the madness, to offer sage advice—but in the end, the complexity of the nightmare is beyond most everyone's skill set. It will take teams of lawyers, therapists, professional contacts, and nonprofit organizations to ever get me out of this mess.

Hugs, your friend, Cindy

The Interrogation

Dear Ken,

You say you are curious about my "feelings" as I navigated through the past years of my life, possibly my lifetime.

My immediate response to this is how could someone *not* know how I felt? How could anyone *not* know how devastating some moments have been and glorious others?

I have stumbled around trying to avoid your question, asking friends and family, "How could Ken possibly need this?" But the answer came back to me time and again: "Cindy, your life is like a movie. People cannot fathom a *year* of it, yet alone year after year after year."

I have asked friends where I should begin and jokingly they said, "July 4, 1958." I reply, "No, seriously." They say, "Seriously! Your life is unbelievable!"

Really what I want to tell you about most are the sweetest, dearest moments I've had with family and friends. Those are my favorite and what I hold most dear, although I know those aren't the stories people like me to tell. But in all honesty, to me there is nothing fascinating or entertaining about being involved in one legal battle and one personal attack after another. After a while it wears you out.

I much prefer to spend time with family and friends, sharing our lives and enjoying each other's company. For some reason, in some way, I have always managed to find a lighthearted moment in most situations. Even those moments when someone holds me as I cry from the horror of details unfolding around me, for some reason, my sense of humor carries me through. There is always something to laugh about.

I have to admit there wasn't much to laugh about when I was asked to go to the police station to be interrogated about the brutal murder of Paul Zimmermann, the father of my children and my husband for 23 years. I guess people would suppose that I would be scared, but I don't recall being scared or frightened.

To my way of thinking I had nothing to hide, so why wouldn't I just go and talk with the police? I'm not a fan of murder mystery novels or movies, so I have limited knowledge about how these things really work. In retrospect, when I think about it, I become more frightened. I look back and think, "Oh my gosh—I could have gone to jail for murder, a murder I didn't commit. A murder that is unthinkable to me."

Yet there were actually people who suggested to the police that I *could* have committed such a heinous crime. How in the world anyone could ever think that is difficult for me to understand. I am still amazed about that as I write this to you, Ken. But the truth is that fingers were being pointed at me.

Here is a quote from the incident/investigation report written by Officer Lockerby on July 22, 2008: "Cindy does lie often." Another quote: "Sarah stated that she asked Kevin if he had felt that Cindy would have anything to do with the disappearance of his father and Kevin had told Sarah that 'I wouldn't put it past my mom to have been involved.' Sarah stated that Cindy does need psychiatric help."

Who is Sarah? The woman Paul had been dating. Who is Kevin? My son. I have no idea whether he actually said those things to Sarah. But I do know his Uncle Mark would use these very quotes against me later in legal documents. I'm sorry, Ken—I am ahead of myself again.

You don't just end up in a police station being interrogated for murder. There are certain events that must happen before you are sitting before several police officers asking lots and lots of questions.

Obviously, someone must be murdered. How in the world this could happen to anyone I know or care about is beyond my wildest imagination. I've never been a fan of guns or violence. As I wrote you before, I didn't allow my children to play even with plastic guns when they were little, or watch violence on television.

Paul, on the other hand, enjoyed murder mysteries and violent-type television programs, although he respected and supported my position to keep guns and violence away from our kids. It is further incredulous to think someone of Paul's intellect and with his expansive reading of murder mysteries would not be aware that he was, in fact, the target of a calculating madman. But that is exactly what happened.

My world, after 23 years of marriage, had become very separate from Paul's. Our long, heated divorce was finally coming to an end. We were waiting for the papers to be signed. Everything was going to be final. We could truly begin our separate lives, with the co-parenting of our children to adulthood to be the final chapter. This was not to be.

I would end up not only single but the sole parent of our children. Sole parenting began for me on Saturday, July 12, 2008, although I didn't know I was a sole parent. Like so many things, I was very unaware of what was going on.

Some people call me "charmingly naïve;" others might use stronger terms, such as just plain stupid. I have had people jokingly comment that I "just might still believe in Santa Claus." No matter the words, even though I knew and those close to the situation knew that Paul was in trouble, none of us could have imagined he was in this *much* trouble.

Saturday, July 12, 2008, I drove to pick my daughter up from summer camp. It was an easy drive, two hours. I was excited to see her. She had been away for four weeks. I knew that she would have stories to share of the special times she had at camp. She loved to go to camp and always had a great time. As a natural conversationalist, it's always been one of my favorite times together, car rides talking and catching up.

Michelle was anxious to return home. She had missed her brothers and father. We arrived back in town. She called her father's cell phone. He didn't answer. She left a heartfelt message. We waited for Paul to return her call.

I wish I could tell you that it was uncommon for Paul not to return phone calls, but in the past two horrific years it had become the norm. We would all leave messages, e-mails, and get little, if any, response. It didn't really seem unusual that he did not race to the phone to talk to Michelle or race to see her.

The days of Paul keeping in close touch with his family and friends had passed several years earlier. He had become very detached from us. We busied our day with settling back in to my casita, unloading Michelle's suitcases, sharing stories of experiences we each had had while apart. But there was that unspoken discomfort that her father hadn't returned her phone call. We went to bed that Saturday night still without a phone call from Paul. But we had the next day to look forward to, as Kevin, her brother, was coming for lunch. We were both looking forward to this. We hadn't had a family lunch in a long time.

We wouldn't be having a family lunch the next day either. Our worlds would never be the same. Our family meals never the same again; we all knew the divorce would change those meals. Long past were the days where we each said the three things we were most grateful for. Long past were the days when we each said what the best thing and the worst thing that had happened to us during our day. That was our family, those were our family meals.

I found new traditions my own way. I attended a spiritual center on Sundays—New Age, some might call it. Maybe a little odd to some, but I liked it. It helped me to live in the moment, be positive, and try to be kind to others. It worked for me, gave

A Woman of Interest

me comfort, and provided what I believe to be a great way to live my life.

On that Sunday I came out of the service feeling particularly happy and renewed. As I mentioned, I was excited to have Kevin over for lunch, and called him to confirm our plans and finalize where we were eating. As it turned out, we weren't going to be meeting for lunch. We were going to be meeting at a police station.

I remember his words vividly. "Mom, I can't go to lunch. I can't find Dad. I'm going to the police station." I asked him, "Police station? Which police station?" He told me, "The Scottsdale Via Linda location." I told him I would meet him there. That's when the surprises began. And we're not talking Santa Claus surprises, at least not the Santa Claus I always believed in.

I immediately drove to the police station, dropped everything, and met my son. Kevin was obviously very, very upset. He had a woman with him who claimed to be Paul's past girlfriend. I wasn't aware Paul had a girlfriend, so while I was a bit surprised, I wasn't jealous or upset.

She would just be the first of a cast of characters new to Paul's life, of whom I had never heard nor met. This new world Paul had created I never cared to enter—one of the reasons my romantic notions for Paul were long gone. I didn't share his fondness for dive bars or the characters who hang out in them. We had gone our separate ways many times when he headed for the dive bars.

Sound snotty? I suppose it does, but that's who I am. I like nice restaurants with white tablecloths, expensive wines, and elaborate food. Paul did, too. He also had affection for dive bars. No matter how many times I begged him to not go to these places, my words fell on deaf ears throughout our marriage. Paul liked playing pool and drinking with guys he met in bars.

I learned that Paul was last seen in one of his favorite watering holes, and that he had been missing since Thursday. This was all news to me. I sat and listened to my son tell the police of how he had been looking for his father. I heard him tell of all the unbelievable things he had done to try and find him.

Here he was, this young 16-year-old son of mine, out looking for his father, like I had done so many times while married to him. I became more and more frightened as my son answered the police officers' questions. I listened, because I had little, if anything, to contribute. I hadn't seen or talked to Paul in a long time.

Rather quickly it became apparent this wasn't a late-night bender, ending up on a buddy's couch. All of those couches had been checked. The favorite bars, the casinos, all checked. All of the obvious and not-so-obvious, the secret places we all go to, had been checked. Paul was nowhere to be found. A panic deep inside my heart began to form as I listened to my son explain the details of Paul's missing days.

In my own way I had tried to give Paul the space he seemed to so desperately want. I had even made the decision on the most recent Father's Day to not wish him a happy Father's Day. It was a tough decision for me, because I loved our shared holidays, and I really wanted the very best for him. I knew being a father was the most important thing in the world to him.

While he wasn't the same father he had been in the years we were together, it was my hope with the divorce behind us he would build his new life and find his way. It was my hope that by not contacting him I wouldn't upset him.

I even wrote in my journal on that Father's Day of my hopes for him. How I hoped he was happy and healthy. I went on to write in my journal I was pretty certain he was.

Then the police told us we could leave and they would start the investigation. I began to make phone calls. Those phone calls no one ever wants to make. The phone calls telling people someone is missing.

I've come to learn that the police give people plenty of time to find their way home; they are used to people and their ways. I've come to learn that when the police tell you to start making

A Woman of Interest

phone calls, it's not good news. So I made the calls. I called my brother, my sister, my son Joe. Joe had left for college in Colorado just four days earlier. I called him to tell him he needed to come home, because the police said he needed to come home. And he did.

I have come to learn that police don't own rose-colored glasses. They see facts, black-and-white facts. Not red, not pretty pink, not baby blue. Facts start to come to light when the professionals become involved with their arsenal of investigative tools.

The first fact: Paul's truck was found. I thought this was great news. While it was news, it wasn't a fact that the truck would bring Paul back home. Second fact: there was a receipt for a storage unit in his truck. Third fact: there were surveillance cameras at the storage unit. The police could view what Paul had been doing.

Paul's new house was the command center, if you will, for the unfolding investigation. The children wanted to stay there so they could be there when he returned home. Mike, Paul's brother, who had flown in from Connecticut, also stayed there. I traveled back and forth from my casita to Paul's house for hourly, daily updates.

Even with guards at the gate, my casita, long my refuge, couldn't keep the media away. One night when I returned, my neighbor, Jessica Youle, came over to tell me reporters had been there. Somehow they had gotten past the guards and were at my front door. She had told the reporters if they came back she was calling her boss, then Governor Janet Napolitano. It doesn't hurt to have friends in high places.

On July 14, 2008, at 6 p.m., it was reported by Officer Lugay of the Scottsdale Police Department that he spoke to me. His incident/investigation report of "Case Number 0820205: The Murder 1st Degree-Premeditated" is similar to my recollection.

I was very uncomfortable answering questions about Paul. I hadn't seen him for some time. In my mind, the family and financial issues had been agreed upon. I just wanted to move my life forward. There wasn't any reason for me to say negative things about Paul. I wanted the best for him.

Our "bests" had become very different, but I didn't think I needed to go into that in the police investigation. When first asked if I was aware of any problems Paul had with drugs, alcohol, or prescription medication, I stated that I wasn't comfortable answering the question.

Officer Lugay informed me that he was just trying to gain information to help in locating Paul. You see, Paul had been missing since Thursday, and it was now Monday. Again I stated, "I do not feel comfortable answering that question."

Officer Lugay: Had Paul ever expressed any intention on hurting himself?

Cindy: Paul has always been very adamantly against that.

Officer Lugay asked me about Paul's current acquaintances.

Cindy: I did not know them…it was only the day before that I had met Paul's girlfriend for the first time.

Officer Lugay: Do you know Terry Brooks or Tommy Sullivan?

Cindy: I just met Terry for the first time the day before at Paul's house. I don't know or never met Tommy Sullivan.

Officer Lugay: Can you identify the person in this picture?

Cindy: Yes, that is Paul. It is his driver's license photo.

Officer Lugay: Do you recognize this person? *(showing another photo)*

Cindy: I don't know who this is.

Officer Lugay:	You don't know this person?
Cindy:	No, I've never seen him before.
Officer Lugay:	Can you tell me the names of your children and their ages?
Cindy:	Yes. Joe, 20; Kevin, 16; and Michelle, 13.
Officer Lugay:	When was the last time your daughter saw her father?
Cindy:	When he dropped her off at summer camp around June 9th.
Officer Lugay:	Where do you work?
Cindy:	I work as a community liaison for Hospice of the Valley.
Officer Lugay:	Where do you think Paul is?
Cindy:	I think that Paul's car got caught in the rain Thursday, his car got in a wreck, he has a bump on his head, and that he needs help.
Officer Lugay:	We have no information that would indicate this scenario.

He went on to tell me the police would notify us as soon as they had any information on Paul's whereabouts.

He next interviewed each of our children, asking them to identify the persons in the pictures. I later learned my children knew the man in the second photo. It was Tommy Sullivan.

We ended the interview at 6:55 p.m.

Next Officer Lugay interviewed Paul's younger brother Mike, who had flown in the night before from Connecticut.

According to the police report, when asked when he last spoke to Paul, his brother stated that he last spoke to Paul a few months ago, and that he used to speak to Paul regularly, but Paul is now "kind of withdrawn."

When asked whether he was aware of Paul abusing drugs or alcohol, his brother said what I had been unwilling to say: "Paul had a drinking problem. I think a lot of it has to do with the divorce."

When asked about Paul's current friends, his brother stated he did not know any of them, though he had spoken to a number of them by telephone in recent hours.

It was awkward being in Paul's new house. I hadn't been in it before, so I felt like an intruder. It was strange to see half of our possessions in this new house. It looked like a typical guy's house. A pool table was placed where a dining room table traditionally stood. His framed Georgetown football jersey, one of the first gifts I had ever given him, was hanging on the wall. A favorite fish he had caught and had mounted from one of his trips to New Zealand graced another wall. All in the dining room.

I remember this because this is where the police spread out photos of people for me and my children to identify. It was beyond bizarre to see photos of different people spread across Paul's much-loved pool table for his family to identify. The kids and I were separated. The police wanted each of us to identify the photos on our own.

While this didn't seem offensive, it just reinforced that we were truly in a police investigative procedure. Not to mention the news trucks outside of Paul's home, the reporters, the yellow tape, and the ever-present police cars. Our family was in the thick of a terrible, terrible nightmare. I will never watch the news or read a newspaper again without an even greater sympathy for the families facing tragedy.

Those photos surprised even the police. We were each separately instructed to look at the pictures and tell them who the people were. The kids knew everyone. I recognized only one, Paul. We were all in agreement which picture was Paul.

For some reason, the police seemed confused that we identified the one particular photo as Paul. We came to find out the police had thought Paul was the person in the footage at the storage unit. The children said, "No, that wasn't Paul—it was Tommy Sullivan."

I remember the police saying, "Are you sure this isn't Paul? This is Tommy?" I didn't know who Tommy was, but I did know the photo wasn't of Paul. The kids knew it was Tommy Sullivan. Who the fuck was Tommy Sullivan? Tommy was one of Paul's new friends. What a friend.

For the police, the investigation unfolded pretty quickly after that. For me, I thought we were still looking for Paul. I reached out to anyone and everyone who I thought might have a clue to Paul's whereabouts. This would prove to be an interesting fact to some people.

It was a *very* interesting fact to the private investigator I called. I reached out to Jon Craig, who now, it seemed, was my personal private investigator. I wanted to hire him to find Paul. He said, "Cindy you are looking out for the wrong person."

I remember asking him, "Really, who should I be looking out for?"

He said, "You need to be looking out for yourself. The police are watching every move you make. You need to get a defense attorney immediately."

"A *what*? Are you kidding me? Why are they looking at me?" I asked him.

"Cindy, you are in trouble," Jon said.

I had no idea. It had never crossed my mind to think about anything other than finding Paul. I followed his advice. I called the recommended defense attorney and he confirmed Jon Craig's words: I was in trouble. It seems spouses—especially spouses who are in the midst of heated divorces and are soon to become ex-wives—are *highly* suspect in missing person cases. Especially when there are people telling the police I was upset about the financial agreement of our divorce and it quite likely could be my motive for this crime. Oh yes, Ken, some day I will share the complete copy of the police report with you.

Now I was going to learn about defense attorneys. I've come to learn defense attorneys want to keep their clients off the stand, away from police officers, away from bolstering their own causes. I guess the theory is that rarely is the defendant the one who can trumpet his or her own innocence. I beg to differ. Oh, you think I'm talking about the murder? Well, yes—I needed a defense attorney for that. But I also needed a defense attorney to defend me against something just as destructive as murder allegations. But more about that later.

But at this time, I still had trouble grasping all of these new developments. I listened closely to the advice of my defense attorney, Robert J. Campos. It was very firm and extremely clear: "Do not, under *any* circumstances, go to the police station without me. Do not allow the police to talk to you without me present. Do you understand?"

Yes, I understood. I wrote a check, putting him on retainer.

Now, in addition to a divorce attorney and an estate attorney, I had a defense attorney. Oh my gosh. What had happened to my life? Long known for gathering information, research, and then doing things my own unique way, this defense attorney was new to my world. Little did he know he had a little fireball on his hands.

The stakes are pretty high when you are asked to go to the police station to talk about whether or not you killed someone. This is the understatement of the year, I suppose. I used my sense of humor to soften my reality—well, that and a few good glasses of chardonnay. Yes I'm a lover of laughter and wine. I figure if I can laugh about it, it can't be all that bad.

The truth is that it really *was* all that bad. It was *really* bad. I remember one therapist saying to me after we had shared a laugh together over a particularly daunting event, "Cindy, this shit isn't funny—it's only funny because you make it funny." But I've learned there is great power in being cheerful, even joyful, in the most desperate of moments.

Here I am, a mother of three wonderful children, weighing my best interests and their best interests, one against the other. I guess it is true: once you hold those babies in your arms, your own interests are a distant second. Even with the stern advice of my defense attorney echoing loudly in my head—DO NOT GO TO THE POLICE STATION WITHOUT ME. DO NOT TALK TO THE POLICE WITHOUT ME—somehow I came to the conclusion that I could best defend myself.

I am fortunate to have my sister and brother live in the same town as I do. We are very close. We respect each other and our differences. Boy, are we different! My sister is a "steady Eddie." While I'm…well I'm *me*! So I've learned in moments that matter to bounce my ideas off of her. Granted, we've both come to know that at best this tends to just slow me down. Sometimes I listen and completely change my path, but for the most part when my heart gets set on something, it's hard for me to change course. Such was my decision to go to the police station alone, without legal representation.

I must pause for a moment and write to you, Ken, of my sister, Gail Kirk. While she is a private person, I will respect her privacy as much as I can, though I am compelled to write of her being my anchor throughout my lifetime. We have shared our lives in a way only sisters can. I am so very, very grateful to her. She has been a rock for my children, as well.

Gail had been by my side throughout the investigation. She was aware that at some point I was going to need to talk with the police about the murder. I remember clearly in one conversation saying to her, "Gail, I don't even remember where I was that Thursday night." She calmly said, "Cindy, I know exactly where you were." That's my sister. Three steps ahead of me most of the time. She can see the trees for the forest. Honestly, I'm generally too busy wandering around enjoying life to think that there could possibly be any need for worry.

Fortunately, I like policemen. I realize some citizens have an adversarial attitude towards police, but I've always found them to be respectful and helpful. I think in some way they are also entertained by the way I interact with them. I am not afraid to be myself, to be authentic. When they are with the police, I imagine most people try to be someone they aren't; maybe better than they might think of themselves. For some reason, I'm perfectly comfortable with my story and myself; it's just another opportunity to share a cup of coffee or conversation with another person.

We had to find Paul. How could we not find him? I had spent 24 years of my life trying to keep him out of his own way. You might also say he did the same for me. We liked to push the envelope. For the most part we did it well and often, though somewhere along the line his "pushing the envelope" became more reckless than I could handle. The stakes were getting higher and higher. Frankly, he scared me. With three young kids to think about, I became more and more resistant to be a part of his behaviors.

On Wednesday, July 16, 2008, at 11:00 a.m., Detective Lugay asked to interview me again. Though I was very confident in my ability to convince the police that I had nothing to do with the murder, I am not completely stupid. I knew enough to have a Plan B. I called my sister and told her I was going to the police station. I wanted someone to know where I was. I gave her two phone numbers, those of my defense attorney and my estate attorney. Being my younger sister hasn't been a walk in the park for her. We are the closest of friends, but surely it hasn't been easy. From a young age, she had to earn her right to hang out with me and my very cool friends! She was a great tagalong and we worked through the normal progression of a relationship that eventually ends on equal footing. I think she might have surpassed me by now. She is a wonderful, dear woman who I adore with all of my heart. Anyway, I called her and told her my plan.

She learned long ago that talking me out of something is fraught with wasted effort. It's better to listen, take notes, and plan either the celebration party or damage control. I was banking on a celebration party. She was putting damage control in place. Unbeknownst to me, she immediately called my defense attorney as I walked alone into the police station to defend myself.

Officer Lugay and I met at the Family Advocacy Center in Scottsdale. He took me back to Interview Room #1 and informed me that he asked me to come in to obtain additional information related to what was now a murder case. I didn't know anything about interrogation rooms. Because I am naturally curious by nature, when entering the room, I was more interested in looking around the room then with the task at hand. I often find other topics to be more interesting than my own, like the badges of honor. When I look at police, I naturally take note of the uniform, but also all of the paraphernalia they have to carry around: the gun, that stick, handcuffs…I don't even know the names of all of the things. It just seems like a lot to carry and keep track of.

The police do not like fun and they weren't interested in having fun with me, although I knew I could tell them the details in a way that would forever reassure them I knew nothing about the death of Paul. My plan was to simply tell them every last detail. Give them names, phone numbers, history, cousins, second cousins. I figured the more details I gave them, the busier I would keep them in verifying those facts and the less time they would spend talking to me again.

My intention was simple. Give them more proof then they could ever need. Give them more research to back up. I've been told that this type of plan literally makes defense attorneys "pee their pants." I swear that's what I was told. What do I know? I didn't need a defense attorney. I didn't do anything against the law, and I certainly did not kill Paul Zimmermann.

In the beginning of the interview, Officer Lugay seemed to be confirming basic information, most of which we had covered before: the years we were married, the ages of our children, our home address, and so forth.

Then he began to ask me questions about our separation and subsequent divorce. Questions I am asked often. If we had such a wonderful life, and Paul was such a wonderful husband and a wonderful father, why were we getting a divorce?

"Things change," I told Officer Lugay. "We were separated On February 17, 2007, and I moved out of the house at that time. Paul had been unemployed since June 2006. During that time, Paul was depressed and started drinking heavily. Over the course of time he began to frequent local bars, such as Goldies, 92nd Street Café, and Teakwoods."

In all fairness to Paul, I must point out that he was very, very successful in his career. He was very dependable and hard working. He was known to be punctual; in fact, he would most generally show up early for appointments, including those with his family. He always thought it was best to be the first one to arrive to a meeting.

In truth, Paul and our family went to Goldies and Teakwoods quite often. They were favorite spots for us to meet other families and friends in the neighborhood. They were nice, upscale sports bars in our community. They were nice places for Paul to watch sports and for me to socialize. We had many good times in these places, but other places Paul liked to frequent were not so nice.

Officer Lugay: Tell me about the incident that prompted your separation?

Cindy: Earlier in February 2007, I was home with our children. My son and I got in an argument. I believed I was being physically threatened by my son. I called Paul and asked him to come home to help manage the situation. Paul told me he was out with his business partners and friends, Dave Van Name and Mark Thomas, and refused to come home to help me. He did not come home until 11 p.m. I had called him for help around 5:30 p.m. To protect myself, I locked myself in our master bedroom. It was this incident that prompted me to get my own apartment, the next day.

I went on to tell Officer Lugay, as I will share with you time and time again, "Up until our separation, we had a wonderful family. Paul was a wonderful father and husband. I still believe the demise of Paul's career was the cause of most of our problems."

As I share this story with you, Ken, it is important to me that you understand that while this incident was a turning point for me and my family, it is not one person, one situation, one incident that undermines a marriage. It was certainly not the fault of my son. He was young, he was frustrated. His father, in my opinion, needed to come home to guide him. Guide him as he had done more times than anyone could ever imagine.

In fairness to Paul, he had always defended me. Paul was also adamant that our children treat me with respect at all times. He did not tolerate them being disrespectful to me, or to anyone else, for that matter. People knew not to mess with our children or me. Paul was quick to defend us, maybe too quick sometimes. The point wasn't really the incident. It was the very, very different way Paul reacted to the incident. Just another reason I knew something was very, very wrong.

Officer Lugay asked me a lot of questions about Paul's current friends. I really had little to share. I told him, "I did not believe any of these people had known Paul for longer than a year."

Officer Lugay	Have you ever met or did you know Tommy Sullivan?
Cindy:	No, I did not know him and had never heard his name prior to this past week.

Officer Lugay:	What is the Tomasio Game Plan?
Cindy:	I don't know what you're talking about.
Officer Lugay:	Do you know Terry Brooks?" (According to the police reports, one of my children stated "this Terry guy" was now Paul's best friend.)
Cindy:	No I don't know him and have never met him.
Officer Lugay:	Do you know or have you ever met another person—something Young, a female name?
Cindy:	No, I have never met her and have never heard of her.

Next, he asked me about the private investigator I hired while we were going through our divorce.

I verified that I had hired an investigator, and gave his name. I explained I hired him shortly after we separated, because I felt Paul possibly was neglecting the children while they were in his care. I had become aware that he left the children alone when he went to the bars. I told Officer Lugay I felt that Paul was not "parenting" in a way that was ideal to me or similar to the way we had generally agreed to parent our children, and that my divorce attorney recommended that I hire a private investigator during the divorce proceedings.

I also shared with Officer Lugay an incident in the report where Paul missed our son's high school graduation, only to find out he was at Teakwoods and 92nd Street Café.

I must reiterate, Ken, that while these were indeed the facts of this particular moment in time, it was so terribly out of Paul's character. Paul—never in a million years, in his right mind—would have missed his son's high school graduation. Absolutely never.

Paul went to most, if not all, of his children's school activities, sporting events, parent teacher conferences, doctor appointments. He was a very involved father. He was well respected by teachers, coaches, fellow parents. He was known to be involved, not just present. He asked intelligent questions in parent teacher conferences. He kept the score book for more baseball/softball games than any father should ever have to. He cooked food on the grill for family and friends. He loved every minute of it. It was his joy.

That is the point. As his wife, I knew that something was changing. Paul was not there to speak for himself. It is certainly not fair for anyone else to speak for him. Was he depressed? Was he tired of the pressure of corporate America? Was it alcohol? Was it our marriage? Our divorce? Simply put, I just don't know, didn't know, and quite possibly will never know. I did know, however, that Paul and my children, when they were with him, were living a lifestyle very different from the one we shared together for more than twenty years. Of course this would be the case in a divorce, but there was something more going on with Paul.

> Officer Lugay: Do you have a copy of the private investigator's report?
>
> Cindy: Yes.
>
> Officer Lugay: Will you give us a copy?
>
> Cindy: Yes.
>
> Officer Lugay: Did Paul know about the private investigator?
>
> Cindy: Yes, he found out about it during the divorce proceedings. He was very unhappy and upset about it. He told our children about it. They were very upset with me. I was seen as the "bad guy" in the divorce.

Officer Lugay:	What do you mean "bad guy?"
Cindy:	This is what I mean about being "the bad guy." Once Paul found out I had called his family, he was very upset. He told me to leave them alone. Paul shared all of this with our children. They were all very upset with me. Because of this phone call and the private investigator, they thought I was being mean.
Officer Lugay:	Were you?
Cindy:	I just wanted the children to be safe and wanted Paul to get better. I know one of my sons in particular is very protective of his father and hides a lot from me.
Officer Lugay:	Phone call? What do you mean by that?

I explained to Officer Lugay that I was trying to do anything I could think of to get Paul help. I had anguished over calling Paul's family asking for help for many weeks. We were not family anymore; we hadn't spoken or seen each other for a long time. I debated with my sister for weeks about calling Paul's brother Mark. I thought Mark was a reasonable person who I could reach out to in a calm, non-confrontational fashion. My family generally stayed in his home when we traveled to Connecticut over the years. His wife and I were friendly sister-in-laws, our children were similar ages, and we were close, at least from my perspective.

After listening to me debate about making the phone call for many weeks, my sister finally said, "You're going to do it, so you might as well get it done." It was a Sunday morning. I remember it so clearly. I called Mark and asked if I might have a few moments of his time. As I recall, he took a couple of moments to go to a private place to talk. It seemed to me he knew the call was important. It is my recollection that I tried to be calm, loving, and concerned for Paul. Simply, I told Mark, "Paul is in trouble, he needs help." Mark and I talked for about an hour. At one point in our conversation, Mark commented, "Cindy, I think if you'll just sign the divorce papers, Paul would be fine." I said, "Mark, he hasn't worked in two years." Mark responded, "Yeah, well he will as soon as this is all over with." And then he asked, "I'm assuming you had him followed?" I replied, "Yes. Yes I did, Mark."

I closed our phone call by saying, "Mark, let's assume this is all about the divorce. For the sake of argument, at the end of the day, do you want Paul's children to see him in a bar every day?" Mark said he would think about it. We hung up. I was grateful I made the phone call. I thought between Paul's six siblings, their spouses, his parents, somebody could help him. How could I be wrong so many times?

It was not to be. I explained that even my brother, Robert Kirk, had talked with Paul about the bars and his new circle of friends. My brother considered Paul to be his best friend. He had met most of the people in Paul's new circle of acquaintances. Paul's response to my brother: "You sound just like your sister." As Paul had considered my brother one of his closest friends for 25 years, my brother was very hurt, upset, and began distancing himself from Paul.

I wouldn't learn until I spent time with Paul's brother Mike that Mark had told only his parents about my concerns. There weren't 14 adults trying to help Paul.

Officer Lugay:	How do you know Mark didn't tell his family?
Cindy:	When Mike, Paul's younger brother, and I were spending time this past week looking for Paul, I made reference to the phone call I made to Mark asking for help. Mike asked, "What phone call?" When I

explained, Mike told me Mark hadn't even told him I had called. Mike and Mark had a disagreement this week about the phone call. From what I understand, Mark only told his parents. Paul's parents did come out to visit Paul a few weeks later.

Officer Lugay: Do you know the owner of 92nd Street Café?

Cindy: Yes. I know Mike Pastiak and his wife Chris. Prior to our separation, they were neighbors when we lived in our old house in the Hillcrest subdivision. Chris and I were in a neighborhood book club. We socialized a few times as couples. After the separation, I lost touch with them. During our search for Paul, I reached out to Mike and Chris to see if they knew of Paul's whereabouts. Mike called the server who served Paul before he left their bar/restaurant. The server just recalled that he had been there with his friends. Mike Pastiak was kind enough to call me back with that information.

Officer Lugay: Have you ever met Paul's girlfriend, Sarah Peterson?

Cindy: I just met her this past weekend at the police station for the first time. I didn't know Paul was dating anyone until then. I had noticed on credit card accounts nicer restaurant charges to places Paul and I used to go, so I thought maybe there was someone in his life. But I didn't really think about it a lot.

I just hoped at the time that in some way whoever it was could give him some type of peace.

Officer Lugay:	When was the last time you saw or spoke to Paul?
Cindy:	It was sometime in late June.
Officer Lugay:	During your separation, have you been in Teakwoods, Goldies, or 92nd Street Café?
Cindy:	Maybe in Goldies once with my sister for lunch or dinner, but other than that I don't go to those places. I don't want to cross paths with Paul. It is too upsetting to see him." But then I remembered, "Oh, I did go to Teakwoods one time."

Officer Lugay wanted to know about that one time. From my perspective, the interview was going very well. The police asked me questions. I answered them.

"It was a few months back," I told him, "when I was determined to try and do anything to get Paul out of the bars. I don't know how I had come up with this idea. It had to be Plan D, E, or F. But I thought maybe, just maybe, if Paul saw me again he would remember his old life. I purposely went to the bar. It was dark inside, mid-morning. I stood at the door with the light shining in behind me. I knew it would be a flattering light, kind of a silhouette. I knew that at one time Paul found me to be beautiful, adored me, and cherished our family. I thought if I just stood there and looked at him, he would for a moment consider what he was doing and quite possibly become nostalgic for his old life. So I stood there. Didn't say a word. After a few moments, one of the guys around the pool table nudged Paul to look at the woman at the door. He looked over at me. We locked eyes for just a few seconds, but it seemed longer. He looked away, turned his back, and went back to his pool shot."

Paul loved to play pool. His decision was made. This was the life he wanted. But you see, I couldn't see any of the people around the pool table due to the darkness, although they saw me and identified me to the police. As I learned later, the new group of friends collaborated that, in fact, yes, this was the only time they had ever seen me.

The police (which included Officer Lugay and an Officer Salazar) were interested in the last e-mail Paul sent me, the one that said, "Happy Birthday." It had been sent on July 5th at approximately 2 a.m. "Is that accurate?" they asked me.

"Yes, those were the last words we ever exchanged," I innocently confirmed. Little did I know this just might be far from the truth.

(The police knew something I did not. Tommy Sullivan had Paul's computer. I would never know for sure who sent those last words, Paul or Tommy.)

Officer Lugay:	Cindy, when were you first made aware that Paul was missing on Sunday, July 13th?
Cindy:	I talked to my son around noon. We were supposed to have lunch together. He was going to see his sister after her long stay away at camp. I was excited because I hadn't seen him for a long time. When I called him, he told me that we couldn't have lunch. He told me he was going to the police department and that Dad had been missing since Thursday. I told him I would meet him there. My son told me he didn't want me there, that he had things under control. I went to the police department

anyway to meet my son and spoke to the reporting officer.

Officer Salazar: Tell me about your day, Thursday, July 10th.

Cindy: I had a work meeting that morning that lasted until noon. In the afternoon I had a doctor's appointment. I met my sister, Gail Kirk, for a short time in Scottsdale. I got home around 6 p.m. A short time later, two of my friends, Debbie Miller and Jennifer Fletcher, came to my casita. Our usual fourth friend Robin Riccardi didn't join us that night. They drove me to have dinner at my friend Eddie Matney's restaurant, Eddie's House. When we entered the restaurant, we were seated in a booth in the back of the restaurant. I tried to slip in, because Eddie is always so generous in sending complimentary food to the table. I didn't want to impose on him. He saw me from the kitchen and said, "Hi Cindy, I see you trying to sneak in!" He came over to the table and greeted us. We had dinner, staying until about 10:30 p.m., and then we went back to my casita and sat in my living room talking until about midnight. My two friends left around midnight.

Officer Lugay: Are you currently dating?

Cindy: No, I am not. I haven't been on one single date since separating from Paul. There was a misunderstanding about my dating, but no, I don't date. In my first PR job for

Bravo Bistro, Chef Tony Hamati and I made the decision for me to join Meetup groups on the Internet to organize events in his restaurant. Somehow Paul found out about it and told our children, who confronted me about it and were very upset. I explained to them that it was for work. I'm not interested in dating. I'm trying to get my life and the kids' lives sorted out.

Officer Lugay: Where do you think Paul is getting his money?

Cindy: We recently sold our property in Montana and have had limited access to those funds. Paul has been spending money rather recklessly, so it was agreed that the profits from the property would be in a sealed account until our divorce was final.

Officer Lugay: What do you mean recklessly?

Cindy: Just not his usual patterns of handling money. We also sold our home and he had profits from that.

Officer Lugay: Were you aware of a million-dollar life insurance policy?

Cindy: Yes, I was.

Officer Lugay: Who is the beneficiary?

Cindy: I was listed as the beneficiary throughout the course of our separation. Since our

A Woman of Interest

divorce was finalized, the children are now the full beneficiaries of the policy.

(During the probate of the estate, the personal representative would discover that in fact there *was* no life insurance. Paul had been reminded many times by his former business associate to pay the approximate $1,500 premium payment. Unfortunately, the life insurance policy had lapsed, because the payment was never made. It would prove to be just one of the many financial decisions that would have an impact on the estate.)

Officer Lugay: So your divorce is finalized?

Cindy: Well, I don't know for sure.

Officer Lugay: You don't know if you are married or divorced?

Cindy: No, I'm not certain if the divorce papers have been signed by the judge."

(We learned later that the divorce decree was signed by the judge the same day Paul was murdered.)

The police also wanted to know if I watched Paul's house. I found the question to be a little bizarre. But I answered truthfully, "No, I didn't watch his house." I already knew what was going on; I didn't need to further bruise myself to watch the details over and over.

The police asked me again, "You do not watch Paul's house?" "No," I told them.

They asked me if I ever sat outside his house on the phone. Finally, I got what they were asking of me. I said, "Oh, yes I have done that. When I go to pick my children up for my week with them, if I arrive early, I sit in front of the house and wait for the kids. It was agreed I picked them up or dropped them off at 5 p.m. on Sundays." I was cognizant of not trying to be antagonistic towards

Paul with our heated divorce. I tried to be very careful not to add fuel to a fire that was beyond simmering at this point.

"I might be there for 10 or 15 minutes. Since I lived 20 minutes away from his new house, sometimes it made sense to arrive early, make phone calls and wait," I told the police.

Unbeknownst to me, there had been witnesses that had reported this to the police, further pointing the finger at me for being a strong person of interest.

What I learned is that policemen have a job to do. They get information and try to verify the facts and put a puzzle together, unfold the mystery; in this case, a murder mystery. And of course, again, Officer Lugay wanted to know why, if Paul was such a great guy, was I divorcing him?

I responded, "The truth is that Paul and I both tried for many, many years to make our marriage work. We wanted to keep our love alive, and in the final years to stay together for our children. He tried. I tried. I can only speak of the many ways I tried through the many years to be a good wife and partner. Obviously I didn't find the right way."

I elaborated, explaining how I tried to keep up, but trying to keep up with a partner who was twice my size and had ten times the stamina didn't work out well, especially when it came to alcohol. I found myself drunk or in situations I didn't like more and more often. It became my pattern to leave events and parties early to avoid the behaviors that were becoming more and more frequent.

Paul, in my opinion, became more and more aggressive when he drank. I'm sure this aggression came from his frustration with his career, in addition to my distancing myself from him. But I just couldn't keep up. Plus, honestly, I find aggressive behavior unattractive. I'm more attracted to soft, loving behavior. I like sweet movies with happy endings. I like everyone to get to win when I'm playing a game, even the game of life. I want everyone to win. That's why I am so drawn to New Age religion, I don't have to hate anyone or judge anyone, and everyone gets to belong. That wasn't the case with Paul.

He wanted to win. Always. He must be the winner. He must be right. In the beginning of our marriage, we would not speak to each other for weeks as we would hold our positions on the issue at hand; literally, weeks of not speaking to each other living in the same house.

It began to wear me out. I remember apologizing and inwardly crossing my fingers, not really thinking I was wrong, but just wanting this to end, apologizing for things that may or may not have been my wrong. Who cared then? Who cares now? I just wanted peace in my home.

The words of the popular Dr. Phil—"Do you want to be right or do you want to be happy?"—became my mantra. If Paul and I got in an argument, I would say, "I am happy." No doubt with the appropriate sarcasm. I was becoming more and more resentful and unhappy in the life we had created.

Of course, there were always antidepressants. Those drugs always seem to be the answer these days. Numb somebody up—they'll never know if they are happy or not, unless they have a really good friend who calls them on the carpet, a friend who has the courage to say, "Cindy, what the fuck is going on?" I have those kinds of friends, one in particular: Cat J. We've been through thick and thin together. We will be friends as long as we live. She had the courage to say, "Cindy, I'm afraid you're going to die." That was the end of the pharmaceutical numbing up. Things were about to change. It's a funny thing when you start seeing things clearly: you know it's time to leave. It's time to get a divorce. It's time to get my own apartment.

A friend said it to me best: divorcing Paul was similar to trying to divorce the Mafia. He wasn't happy about it and he wasn't going to make it easy for me—and his brother Mark had no trouble picking up the mantra once Paul was gone. Paul was the golden boy. How could he possibly be responsible for any of this? Many people decided it was all my fault. Surely I'm the one who forced Paul to go drink every day with a bunch of guys he'd just befriended.

Oh, let's not even go there. The truth is I felt like I was on the Titanic. The ship was going down. I tried desperately to sound the sirens, to get anyone and/or everyone's attention and to help get my family off of the ship, to let them know our ship was going down. I begged for help. I desperately wanted Paul to "wake up" and come to his senses. It was not to be.

The closest I can describe my feelings is the scene in the Titanic where the band is playing as the ship goes down. Some people just wouldn't stop listening to the music. That was Paul and many of those who didn't want to believe he was on a wayward path. No matter how close you are to someone—in my case, to Paul—there will always be things you won't know and questions that will go unanswered.

I don't recall if I told the police all of these details, but I'm sure I probably summed it up by saying, "The failure of our marriage is not something I like to think about. I would rather focus on the many wonderful memories we shared."

Officer Lugay brought me back from my meandering: "We will probably have to interview your son [Kevin] again sometime in the next few weeks. There are some issues we need to clarify in regard to our first interview with him."

I learned later there was some conflicting information in his interview. I was very concerned and still am to this day the heavy burden on my son and the role this has had to play on his young heart in this investigation.

I asked the officers, "Am I a suspect in this case?"

Officer Lugay: No, you are not. Your interview is very important as you were married to Paul for over twenty years. You probably knew him best out of everyone we have spoken to. Can you provide us a copy of your final divorce settlement?

| Cindy: | Yes, I will give you a copy. I'm happy to give you any paperwork or documentation you need. |

| Officer Lugay: | Do you know what the tentative funeral arrangements are for Paul?" |

| Cindy: | There may be a small service after he is cremated, with his ashes going to Montana. |

(In the end, Paul had a service with many friends and family. At his parents' request, his ashes were buried in a cemetery near their home in Stuart, Florida.)

I had a question of my own: "May I ask you about Paul's physical condition? How did he die?"

| Officer Lugay: | The medical examiner is conducting the autopsy. I don't have any additional information as to how Paul died. |

| Cindy: | How long will it be until we know the autopsy results? |

| Officer Lugay: | We will follow up with you later this week. |

| Cindy: | Ok, thank you. |

The interview was concluded at 12:15 p.m. I had accomplished what I had set out to do: defend myself.

I left the police station alone and returned to my car to a phone that was overloaded with urgent messages. And the message weren't from people cheering me on. They were from people praying I had come out safe and sound. People scared to death for me. That's what happens when you have to face the police who suspect you might have murdered someone. I guess the police station *is* kind of a scary place to go on your own.

The most important message was from my defense attorney. To say he was not pleased is yet another understatement. His message was simple: "Call me immediately as soon as you come out of that police station."

The phone may have rung one time before he answered. I remember clearly his words: "You don't listen very well, do you?"

I explained my decision. To my way of thinking, the most important jury was comprised of my three children. Had I gone into the police station with a defense attorney, then I must have something to hide. My children were being fed nasty information about me. My focus was on my children first. They had to process their father being missing and most likely dead by foul play, and now the possible murderer being their mother. I could at least take the second horror off of their minds, or so I thought. Again, I had nothing to hide, so why not go to the police station?

"Because, Cindy, anything you said in that police station can be used against you. I will not have access to the information," my defense attorney told me. "We'll get through it, don't worry. Now tell me exactly what you said." And I tried to retell it to him, to the best of my ability.

His response: "Oh, Cindy."

I chose how to handle my interactions with the Scottsdale Police Department. After much thought and consideration given to the advice of not going without a defense attorney, I made the decision to cooperate fully with the police openly throughout the disappearance and investigation of my children's father, Paul Zimmermann.

I will never be able to say enough about the professional, respectful, dedication the Scottsdale Police Department showed me and my family. I will be eternally grateful for their learned skills in solving this heinous crime. I am grateful to the taxpayers of my community, as we all fund the departments that investigate missing persons (of course, none of us ever expects it will be *our* family that needs the services the most).

You can imagine, Ken, I am exhausted from writing this letter to you. It is certainly a unique experience, but it is so painful to revisit and almost impossible to imagine it really happened.

I must go for my hike now. Hugs and more hugs, your friend, Cindy

THE AFTERMATH

Dear Ken,

It seems I have been "reacting" rather than acting upon my dreams and passions. A person long known for making lists and achieving goals, I could more easily relate to writing a book about medical sales as I had a long career in the medical world. Or maybe writing about investments, as I'm naturally interested in that. But a book about attorneys and police interrogations? This is not my forte, Ken. But I will try and write you of this time in my life.

I will try because you asked me to. I like to try to do what people ask of me. I trust you. We have mutual friends who I trust and respect. Therefore, it seems natural for me to trust you.

Trust seems to be a deep thread in my personality. I am comfortable trusting. I like to trust. I had trusted my husband to provide for my children and me. I had trusted him to be a good father and husband, to put our interests as a family before all others. For many years he had. In the end, we had come to agree on our divorce. Neither of us was happy, but we had an agreement.

I still had much to deal with ahead of me. One unexpected challenge came towards the end of 2008, and lasted until November 2011. Would this nightmare *ever* stop?

The easy part of a divorce is dividing assets. In Arizona everything is split 50/50. That should seem easy enough. It wasn't easy for Paul and me. It wouldn't be easy for the personal representative of the estate.

Anything with emotion can be difficult. Ironically, I thought we were dividing assets. Accounting and money is pretty black and white to me. Back in the '90s I had even led women financial groups, helping women learn the very basics about their personal finances. I was and still am surprised when I learn anyone—but women in particular—can be prone to resisting managing their finances.

Thankfully, I was always very involved and informed with our financial information. I would need to be to get through the next few years. I must give credit to my mother for this. From a very young age she taught me how to manage money. She worked for H&R Block when I was a young girl. The IRS, taxes, and audits were common words in our home.

My parents divorced when I was in the 4th grade. I saw first-hand my mother manage the pressure of raising young children on limited funds. It must be because of this that I have always had an interest in generating income. I am not comfortable wasting money or resources and have a healthy regard for savings and wise investments. Foolish financial endeavors do not sit well with me.

Our financial details were complicated, but as it would unfold with the estate, the mounds of documents, explanations, and witnesses brought forth to attempt to explain our finances wouldn't make any difference. It would prove impossible for others to grasp the details, or at least my version of the details. As I would come to learn, even things that can seem black and white have shades of gray in them.

What could happen next? What in God's name could happen next? My life couldn't get any worse. There *couldn't* be any more challenges. I was up to my neck in to-do lists, barely sleeping, trying to care for my children, trying to keep my job, trying to answer the personal representative's many requests. Trying to figure out what was what. Then the IRS wrote me. They wanted $25,000. You've got to be kidding me. An audit? Now?

I wrote Betsy Rollins, my auditor, a long letter explaining that this wasn't really a good time for me to be audited. I explained in great detail. Betsy—or, more accurately, the IRS—didn't care. They wanted their money or they wanted me to prove why I didn't owe the money.

Since Paul had passed away, the defense of the $25,000 obligation would fall on my shoulders. His expenses after my explanation to the IRS would not be scrutinized. Only my expenses and those of my company, Writing In Style, would need to be reviewed, although the estate and I were equally financially responsible for the payment. I would be the one obligated to prove our 2006 tax return was accurate.

After two moves, two storage units, and kids moving in and out, finding the receipts and details was just overwhelming. I also have this belief that once the IRS starts auditing, they don't stop. So I knew I had to give them the information they needed and not just write a check. Not to mention the fact that I was not really interested in writing checks for $25,000 for things I didn't owe.

Again, I had a dear friend help me. How do you ever thank a friend who donates a long weekend to come to your house to organize tax records, type the details up, and get them ready for the IRS? I don't know the answer. But I am eternally grateful to Barb Dillman. Barb and I had been friends for years, as had our husbands, who worked together with their common interests in sports medicine. To me, Chuck is a friend, and a delightful man. To many, he is Charles J. Dillman, Ph. D., well respected for his years involved with the Olympics as the Assistant Executive Director for the U. S. Olympic Committee and on the International Olympic Committee's Medical Commission. It is important to me that I not disrespect his lifetime of accomplishments because of my familiarity with him. Anyway, international traveling with friends, as we often did with this wonderful couple, either strengthens or breaks a friendship. Barb, Chuck, and I will be friends for life.

There's something about being around famous, powerful people. There are lots of egos and agendas. It's nice to have a girlfriend to compare notes. Barb and I always had each other's backs and understood the "game." We were known for our entertaining and boy, did we entertain! Barb and I have shared life's ups and downs, joys and celebrations. I wouldn't have survived without her.

She insisted on coming out to help me with the IRS audit. Having someone help you with your financial stuff is tricky. One, money does strange things to relationships. Two, taxes and tax returns are complicated. Heaven only knew what we would find.

In our early marital days, I was very organized financially. I was the kind who used color-coded highlighters to balance my checkbook. Paul was different. He thought tossing everything into a box and "guessing" at numbers was a better way to manage our finances. This difference would prove difficult through our divorce as well.

As with any marriage, you learn to choose your battles. I followed his lead on how to manage our taxes. So each year at tax time, we would get our box out, open a bottle of wine, and make some sense of the papers. Then we'd make our appointment with our tax accountant, a family friend named Terry Sarvas, CPA of Sarvas, Coleman, Edgell & Tobin, P.C. We would walk in with our box of papers and he would just shake his head. We had our usual 20 minutes of catching up on family, mutual friends, and then our work began, putting the numbers together for our tax return.

Terry Sarvas is an ethical accountant. He made sure we didn't do anything inappropriate, although I'm sure our method of madness wasn't too impressive from an accounting standpoint. He had also seen the dynamics of our marriage through these appointments for many, many years and had witnessed Paul's demise. He had seen how difficult it was to get Paul to do his taxes or even function the year we were separated, divorcing. He was concerned for our family, too.

When the audit came, Terry was stunned. He didn't know how much more I could take. To make matters worse, the personal representative of the estate had been badgering Terry for information that was inappropriate and out of line. He was one of my many firewalls. He knew how much pressure I was under. But I had to get the information together and respond.

Barb flew out to help me. Barb and I have shared many wonderful girlfriend vacations together. We are used to each other's style. I remember when she first entered my casita, filled with my children (and one of Kevin's friends, who needed a place to stay) and our scattered belongings, she said, "Cindy, this is craziness. There are kids and things everywhere. The house is a mess. You have a teenager living here who isn't even your child. What are you doing?"

"Yes," I told her, "I know. I have no choice." I explained that my home wasn't the tidy, well run ship of days gone by. We were all just trying to right the world of ours that had been turned so terribly upside-down.

After a couple of nights of trying to sleep, she took me aside and said, "Cindy, people are up all night. You aren't sleeping. Things are out of control." "Yes," I said again, "I know." I was trying to choose my battles. First and foremost, the home was a safe haven where my kids could grieve and hopefully thrive again. With teenagers, and such tremendous grief, we all had to process in our own way. We talked, we cried, we stared hypnotically at the TV, but mostly we grieved. Whatever, we were each finding our own way.

Somehow, some way, my angel Barb and I got the receipts, the timeline, the details in order for the IRS. I am grateful with all of my heart to Barb for helping me and for keeping my financial information between us. We sent the information to my new friend Betsy, who would not be so easily satisfied. She wanted more.

Honestly, this went on for two years. Request after request after request; $6,000 in accounting fees. I know my accountant was generous with his time and fees. The estate wouldn't pay for any of the expenses, so in addition to coping with all of the physical details of the audit, I also had to fund the accounting fees.

Money was flying out of my savings like there was no tomorrow. Nobody seemed to care, except for my dear family and friends.

A Woman of Interest

They cared a lot. They loved me a lot. They wrote me cards. They did everything they could to try to keep me strong. But there were some things I could only do myself. I was the only one who had the information.

Finally, I said, 'Enough." No more accountants. I wanted a face-to-face audit with the IRS. My accountant thought I had lost my mind. Maybe I had. I felt certain if I could just explain to someone about Writing In Style and my love of the handwritten note, they would understand. It is hard to understand why someone would spend so much time and money on the handwritten note. I get that. But I can explain it, I promise!

I got my appointment. This made my family and friends nervous, too. When you decide to go to the IRS without representation it makes people very nervous. It didn't make me nervous at all, because I had nothing to hide. In fact, I decided to take my daughter with me. I wanted her to see firsthand that there is nothing to be frightened of when an entity or authority asks for you to explain your behavior, your business. You just ask for an opportunity to explain in a respectful manner. That's really all you need to do.

I loaded up my suitcase of everything I could imagine my new IRS friend Kimberly might want to know about Writing In Style and the handwritten note, and off we went. It was a purple suitcase that matched my logo.

To be perfectly honest, I was kind of excited. A little nervous, but more excited that I was going to get to talk about the handwritten note for three hours! This was exciting stuff—you see, I love to talk about the handwritten note. Also, because my mother had so often talked matter-of-factly about the IRS when I was young, the agency didn't hold the same fear for me as maybe it does for others.

We arrived at the IRS headquarters at 9 a.m. I put on my cheery smile and promptly asked Kimberly if she had ever written with a fountain pen. I pulled one out and asked her if she would like to try. I swear I really did this. I also learned that she had a daughter and she hadn't ever written with a fountain pen. So, I could tell we were making headway with the audit.

Kimberly thought differently! I sensed that she, if not entertained with my presentation of information, was intrigued. Clearly, I had a passion for the handwritten note. It was a Friday. I was hoping to have her week and mine end on a positive note.

Passion isn't worth $25,000, and she certainly wasn't going to just wipe away the questions that needed to be answered. I had to prove it. Prove it I did. With each question, I tried to have what you might call a "show and tell" type of response. I wanted her to remember this audit and frankly quite possibly become yet another advocate of the handwritten note. This was most likely an audit like no other Kimberly would ever have. I described in vivid detail the lengths to which I went to share my passion with others, from creating a professional DVD to explain the history and value of the handwritten note, through events laden with interesting activities and local celebrities and more. I'm fairly certain she could only imagine what was going to come out of my purple suitcase next!

Though the morning was beginning to run long, there was one last subject Kimberly wanted to ask about. I remember it vividly. She wanted the receipt for my computer: $1,500. That was a big chunk of the $25,000. I looked through all of my papers and I couldn't find it. I explained to Kimberly that this computer was only used for my Writing In Style business. It was a big family issue because I didn't want viruses on the computer. The kids knew all about this family rule, and my daughter verified this. But Kimberly needed a receipt. All of a sudden, it dawned on me. I kept it in my computer bag, in case I ever needed to return it to the store where I had purchased it. So, I reached in my computer bag and proudly handed it over to Kimberly. I will never forget my daughter saying, "There is a method to her madness!" We all laughed.

After three long hours, we were about halfway through my purple suitcase of receipts and "show and tell." Kimberly had another appointment, but she said she would make another appointment for me. As I recall, she explained to me that this was highly extraordinary. But if I went home and organized my receipts and papers in a different fashion, she would give me one more appointment. I agreed.

The next appointment was about numbers only, with no visual effects or demonstrations. We shook hands or I probably hugged her, as I like to do. I thanked her very much for her time and told her I would look forward to our next appointment together.

I prepared for my next appointment precisely the way she requested. I presented the information in a more traditional manner. The audit was over. I owed $1,500. I went from $25,000 to $1,500. Even my accountant was impressed, although he did tell me he would have fired any other client who dared to represent themselves in an IRS audit.

From my perception, that visit to the IRS will be one of my fondness memories shared with my daughter.

It seemed like a happy ending, but get this: the IRS can take money out of your accounts without your permission. Somehow, they decided to take $10,000 out of my savings account. All that work, and they *still* took $10,000. It took me about four months, but I finally got an explanation for that. When they wrote the refund check of $10,000, they sent it to the estate. The estate took that money from me, too! The check was endorsed and held until we went to court. Eventually, the estate paid half of the $6,000 in accounting fees and gave me back my $10,000. This all happened in November 2011. It started in October 2008. Three years. IRS audit completed.

But the most difficult challenge was yet to come.

Being on the witness stand is not like having a conversation. Listen to the question, answer it, and stop talking. Don't offer follow-up or clarification. If you don't understand something, say so. If you don't remember something, say so. If you get confused say, "I don't recall." That's how my attorney trained me.

I wouldn't end up on the stand for murder, but rather to remove the personal representative who was managing Paul's estate, his brother Mark, my ex-brother-in-law. This was a next-to-impossible feat to accomplish.

It was hard for me to believe after everything my three children and I, our family, had been through, there would be more. Not from the police, but from family.

It was hard for me to believe that after facing question after question from the police during the murder investigation that the personal representative of the estate wouldn't consider our family had been through enough. It was not to be.

I've come to learn that it's extremely difficult to navigate the world of attorneys, and found that many seemed to be "in it for the money," although, honestly, Ken, it never crossed my mind that that was what attorneys were about. I was fortunate to find attorneys who were professionals.

I looked to Steve Smith, my divorce attorney, to navigate my prolonged divorce. I was in way over my head trying to stay one step ahead of Paul and his new ways. It seemed to be one crisis after another. I trusted Steve to help me, guide me, to care for me. I believe he did.

In the last months of 2008, my estate attorney Diane Prescott and I started to re-evaluate our working relationship. We had tremendous respect for each other. She had helped me update my personal will, my living will, and had reviewed my divorce decree. She is an excellent attorney, a woman of true character. But I was going to need a different attorney, an attorney who specialized in aggressive probate cases. I put my tail between my legs and went to my neighbor's house again (as you may recall, this was the neighbor who worked for then Arizona Governor Janet Napolitano). I trusted her.

"Can you help me?" I asked. "Do you know of an attorney that can help me?" She did. George Paul of Lewis and Roca, LLP, was the attorney I should hire.

So I met with George Paul. I didn't have the foggiest idea that he was one of the leading legal philosophers of the day. He had written famous books and articles, was the Chair of several national committees, and the law professors and judges were studying what he said and quoting his books in their own articles—even in briefs before the U.S. Supreme Court. He had been a delegate at the United Nations, when countries were deciding how to build a sustainable future. That was not my world with George. I did not know that such a world even existed. We didn't even talk about it! I was clueless. I have since come to learn that he lives a sort of double life, about which I was unaware.

Instead, I saw George as my champion. He was fighting for me. He was going to kick ass! He was a superb trial lawyer. He was recognized as a "Super Lawyer," not because of his deep thinking, but because he could tear people apart in court. He was recognized in "Best Lawyers in America," had all the ratings and credentials, and was in the top five in his class at Dartmouth and at Yale Law School, and on and on—because of his trial skills, and his knowledge of intellectual property, trade secrets, and things technological. Above all else, he seemed to care about me as a person. He was standing up for me, and explaining how the system worked, so that I would not be ruined by the forces opposing me.

From my viewpoint, I had tried to work with Mark as best I could. I responded to mounds of daily e-mails requesting various tasks to be completed; this while I was trying to mother my children, work at Hospice of the Valley, and manage my own grief. But the cooperative relationship between my former brother-in-law and me wouldn't last long. About a month, in fact.

Our cooperative relationship ended the day he asked me to destroy the original will and testament of Paul's estate.

It gets better. I almost did it.

Truly, I almost did it. Mark is an attorney—surely, he knew best, I thought.

Having second thoughts, I called Diane Prescott, my police advocate Natalie Summit, and my sister to discuss the shredding of the will. They unanimously said, "Are you nuts?"

The pressure began from many fronts for me to immediately file a bar complaint against Mark Zimmermann. It was a decision that was very difficult for me. I just could not comprehend that the man who had been my brother-in-law for 23 years, who had hosted me and my family as a guest in his home more times than I could count, would act in a way that was seemingly not in my or my children's best interests. We shared many holidays, vacations, good times…at least as I remember them. I liked him, I trusted him.

Time and time again, I was advised, "Cindy, you must file a bar complaint." It is absolutely professional misconduct for a lawyer to engage in conduct involving dishonesty, fraud, deceit, or misrepresentation. I resisted until September 28, 2009. I did not want to do him harm. I still do not want to do him harm.

In the bar complaint I submitted to the State of Connecticut Judicial Branch, my attachment read:

"Nature of Complaint: Mark J. Zimmermann committed professional misconduct by encouraging and pressuring me to destroy the original of my deceased ex-husband's will. Under Rule of Professional Conduct 8.4(3), it is professional misconduct for a lawyer to engage in conduct involving dishonesty, fraud, deceit, or misrepresentation. I also believe that by encouraging me to destroy a testamentary instrument, Mr. Zimmermann may have committed a criminal act that reflects adversely on his honesty, trustworthiness or fitness as a lawyer, which is professional misconduct under Rule 8.4(2)." The Attachment A went on to describe the details of Mark Zimmermann requesting me to destroy the original will. I closed my attachment requesting "that my complaint be forwarded to a grievance panel for investigation."

July 2, 2009, almost a year later, and Mark had dragged out the probate. In my opinion he was trying to bankrupt me and alienate me from my children.

Many tens of thousands of dollars later, I got a letter from George Paul. He called it a "Stop, Look, and Listen" letter. He used words like "catastrophe," "worst case scenario," "catastrophic." Clearly, the "Stop, Look and Listen" letter said if I lost the case, the results would be catastrophic.

I didn't plan on losing. Mark would be removed as the personal representative of the estate, at all costs. "Poison in my family's drinking water" is how my family therapist described him to me. My police advocate warned me to "watch out" for this guy. Finally, I listened. No more benefit of the doubt for my ex-brother-in-law.

George Paul wanted me to have a letter that somewhat formally set forth the risks—particularly in this "odd fact pattern" that made it seem like I was fighting against my own children. It wasn't just me. Mark was doing this to his brother. In my opinion, he was not following his brother's wishes for this estate, but rather was following his own agenda. It was no coincidence that when I met George, he introduced himself George Paul. He said, "I hope you don't mind, I have a young attorney who I'd like to witness this complicated case. His name is Josh Zimmerman."

I didn't mind at all. I knew that was Paul's way of telling me we were still a team, parenting our children. We would win. We were a power couple again. Mark was an easy foe. Why? He couldn't shut his mouth. He thought he knew me. He was wrong.

How could she? How could she rip my mother's day book out of my hands to make copies of my children's letters to me? Because she could; that's what happens in depositions. Sharon Moyer of Sacks, Tierney, P.A., was the attorney my ex-brother-in-law hired to represent the estate. You will learn more of her, Ken, when I write you later about the court trial.

I treasure my mother's day book of letters from my children. Years ago, I asked them if each year they would write a letter to me. They did. Paul always made certain they put pen to paper. I liked them because they captured where our relationship was at the time, what they had valued and remembered of the previous year. It had become an important family tradition.

I had taken it to the deposition as a security blanket. I would use the day book as a visual aid to remind me that every word I said must be in the best interest of my family. The stakes were high and obviously the competition was stellar.

The court reporter was stunned. George Paul was stunned. They both claimed they had never seen anyone be so mean in a deposition. The message was clear; the gloves were off.

Mark liked to play games. Let the games begin. But we needed a game plan. Sensibility wasn't working, and my attorney fees were mounting up with no progress made.

I wasn't worried or intimidated; George Paul had prepared me well. "They are going to beat you up. Can you go in the ring and take a beating?"

"Yes," I told him, "I can."

Our plan was this: let opposing counsel beat the shit out of me. All we had to do was prove that the personal representative and I couldn't get along. We didn't have to prove whose fault it was. It wasn't about proving who was right or who was wrong. We didn't have to prove anything except that we couldn't get along. By law, I had rights to be treated civilly in probate.

George trained me well. We spent a great deal of time preparing for the time I would be in court on the witness stand. George educated me that this is where many attorneys and clients lose cases; their client not being prepared for the stand. He also said many clients don't understand the value of the investment. It was expensive, but this was all or nothing. My family was at stake.

To be honest, the only thing I would need to manage would be my emotions. I must maintain my composure. This was *not* my day in court. The opposing counsel would have no difficulty playing their part. Opposing counsel was a perfect team. Demeaning and treating me with disrespect would come naturally, in my opinion.

Of all the things I valued most, the parenting of my children was absolutely the most important thing to me. Throughout all of my family's trials and tribulations, I tried to keep my children's best interests at the forefront. I've never held the belief that I am the best mom in the world or the only person that could love them and nurture them to success.

I have read mountains of parenting books throughout my time as a parent. I did the very best I could. But somehow my best was twisted into horrible, near "Mommy Dearest," proportions. Our children were beginning to flounder. Eighteen years of parenting seemed to be coming undone at an unbelievably fast pace. To say it was heartbreaking is an understatement.

Parent alienation. Do you know of it, Ken? It's one thing to have my character challenged by a friend; well, he or she wouldn't be a friend now, would they? It's another thing to have my children alienated from me.

To those who knew our family, the accusations were beyond belief. That's why it's called "parent alienation." Honestly, I think to those who cared about me and still care about me that the "circumstances" were more frightening or frustrating for them than me. To an outsider it seemed like madness, which it was. To me, the insider, I trusted the courts, my attorney, and the professionals to help me. It was not to be.

At the time of the divorce proceedings, slowly and methodically, Steve, my divorce attorney, would introduce or suggest the next thing we needed to do to bring our marriage to an end. They were very, very difficult and agonizing decisions. Always most important to me were our children. They were to Paul, too.

The same was true of Diane Prescott and George Paul, my estate attorneys. We tried to execute the divorce decree. It seemed it would never, ever end. My family felt the same.

Parent alienation happens little by little. Honestly, I don't think Paul knew he was doing it intentionally. I think he was lost, very lost. It began with Paul using the children almost as personal therapists. He would talk with the kids with great specificity about our marriage and our divorce. Yes, even our love life. I was stunned. He was always such a private man. How could he do this?

The dance began when he told the children untruths about me, and then they naturally asked me if the untruths were true. This dance will most likely continue throughout my lifetime. There are others who have carried on the dance with my children. The partner may change; the dance does not.

That is the poison of parent alienation. Once a parent is alienated it is difficult, almost impossible, to undo the damage.

It has been said that nothing stirs up passions more than parents at war over the custody of a child. I would have to agree with this wholeheartedly. Paul and I both loved our children very much. We had devoted 18 years of our lives to raising them. We endured high-risk pregnancies to bring them into the world. They were deeply loved by both of us.

But then fear overtakes reason. Incomplete facts become evidence. Court calendars become jammed with repeat visits to a judge to try and bring sanity to what is unlikely to ever be untangled. Then begins the child's (or children's) campaign of denigration against a parent; a campaign that has little or no justification. I wish I could say my family was exempt from this, but it wasn't the case.

Ken, from my research and counseling, I have arrived at several guideposts for rebuilding my family or me living a somewhat sane, happy life:

I will not live a victim's life. I will try to understand the nature of my challenges, but not get caught up in how terrible they might be. I've come to learn this type of judgment is what can bring a person down emotionally.

Very importantly, I will not show my children court orders or other sensitive documents. I will not allow my children to overhear

A Woman of Interest

inappropriate conversations on the telephone. I will never ask nor allow my children to testify for me in court.

I will not talk disparagingly about their father or his family, which is why some of this is difficult to write about. Unfortunately, court documents speak for themselves. I will seek to reinforce positive memories, of which there were many. I will not join in a new custody battle with debates over holiday celebrations and so forth. I will support each of my children in the way they feel most comfortable in these celebrations and passages.

I will focus on enjoying my children's company and not talk to them about the negative experiences we have had to navigate. Having said this, I will not allow my children to treat me with disrespect. We are navigating our relationships from that of mother/child to adult/adult.

I will not violate court orders. I paid my child support on time, completed my required parenting classes, and proved to live within the letter of the law.

I will always call or show up to see my children, even if I know it might be uncomfortable or they might not be excited to see me. No matter how disappointed or painful it might be, in my heart I will know that I tried to see them.

I will try to be a truly decent, principled person and make it obvious I love my children. I will not allow the opinions of others to upset me.

While I have certainly thought of giving up, I would not, will not. No matter how awful the harassment, I will not give up on the goodness of my children, my family.

I will to go to the financial expense of seeing it through. If necessary, I will go as far to represent myself in court without an attorney to protect my family.

To the best of my ability I will try to be even-tempered, logical, and keep my emotions under control. I will surround myself with friends and family that support my attitude. I do not want to retaliate or act in anger. My anger will only prove that I am unstable.

I will try desperately to avoid adding to the problem. Many times I don't know how to make it better, but I certainly know what makes it worse.

And finally, some days I will close the doors to my casita, open a bottle of wine, count my blessings, surround myself with handwritten notes and just plain call it a day. But not the end, because, as one of my favorite greeting cards reads, "In the end everything is okay. If it's not okay, it's not the end."

Hugs and more hugs, your friend, Cindy

UNDER OATH

Dear Ken,

I think it's best to let the court transcript, a public record, speak for itself. I briefly mentioned to you previously how my attorney, George Paul, prepared me for this day.

As we began, George leaned over to me and said, "I'm so sorry. Are you ready?"

"Yes," I replied, "I am ready."

October 6, 2009

Judge: We are proceeding at this time to PV 2008-002158. This is an action related to the underlying estate of Paul Thomas Zimmermann. Specifically this afternoon we are proceeding to evidentiary hearing on the petition filed to remove the personal representative for cause and for other relief. This petitioner seeks the removal of the current personal representative, Mark Zimmermann, and the record further reflects that Mr. Zimmermann was informally appointed personal representative pursuant to the terms of the 22-page will back on August 19, 2008. So let's begin by having the parties please announce for the record.

George: May it please the court, my name is George Paul from the firm of Lewis and Rocca and I represent Cindy Zimmermann, who is a creditor and an interested party and the mother of the three beneficiaries of the will and the testamentary trust.

Sharon: I am Sharon Moyer, representing Mark Zimmermann as the personal representative of the estate.

Judge: Okay, great. Now I did have an opportunity to review the file before proceeding today to evidentiary hearing. And I also reviewed the trial brief. I have not yet of course had an opportunity to review the matters marked as exhibits in this manner... we are proceeding on the petition for removal of the personal representative as a result of this matter being filed by the petitioner, Cynthia Kirk Zimmermann. I will at this time go to you, Mr. Paul, did you wish to make any opening statements regarding the relief you are seeking?

George: Yes, your honor, and some evidence.

Judge: The relief you're seeking on the basis.

Sharon: Can we exclude witnesses, please?

Judge: Let me explain, certainly. Ladies and gentleman, the rule regarding the exclusion of witnesses has been invoked. What that basically means is that with the exception of these specific parties, and or any agents of the parties any other individuals who may be called to testify, will be asked to remain outside of the courtroom while the other witnesses are testifying, and you are hereby informed and directed not to discuss your testimony or the testimony of any other witnesses until after you have concluded your

A Woman of Interest

testimony. Once your testimony is provided, I will give you the opportunity to either be excused if you so elect or to remain in the court for the balance of the proceedings. So I guess the issue then is, who do you anticipate calling who would be subject to the rule regarding the exclusion of witnesses?

Sharon: Well, I only have Mr. Zimmermann and I have Kevin Zimmermann, who is going to appear telephonically.

Judge: Okay, to testify?

Sharon: To testify. I truthfully don't know who the other people in the courtroom are. So, I don't know if they are witnesses or not.

Judge: Mr. Paul, any other individuals in the courtroom that you anticipate calling as witnesses?

George: Excuse me. *(Question to Cindy.)* Why don't we just excuse all three of them, because they are potential witnesses.

(My sister Gail Kirk, attorney Diane Prescott, and close friend Mike Oleskow had all come to court to support me and take the stand to testify if need be. They would wait in the hallway all morning, wondering what was happening to me, never to re-enter the courtroom.)

Judge: Okay, I hate to do it to you, but if you want to step outside into the corridor, then as the hearing progresses we will let you know immediately when your testimony is sought. Now, I haven't received a call yet from Mr. Kevin Zimmermann. Were we going to wait until the appropriate time to call him?"

Sharon: That's what I was thinking, since I assumed we would exclude anyways.

Judge: Okay.

George: Well, your honor, with Kevin Zimmermann, [although] there was a request for telephone deposition, I've never seen someone testify at a trial, at a hearing.

Sharon: The court ordered that it was permitted.

George: By telephone, okay.

Judge: I frequently do authorize that and…I do it with great hesitation because it creates problems. Not only for the witness, but also to counsel. But generally, I will authorize it in those circumstances where we do have someone out of state.

George: Okay, that is fine.

Judge: And that's why I authorized it. Now I don't necessarily do that for the parties if they may be from out of state, but I have had the misfortune on one occasion of having eight hours of testimony.

George: On telephone?

Judge: Telephonic. So I do it in a very hesitant fashion, but really more as a courtesy.

George: Okay, that's fine. It's your ruling. I've just never seen it before.

Sharon: I promise it won't be eight hours.

Judge: Yes, and I'll tell you ahead of time, too, that they have a really ancient phone system here in the courtroom. So when a witness appears telephonically, that means I am going to be directing counsel to step forward, because I can't move the phone. So it practically creates some difficulties, but we can overcome them for short testimony.

Judge: Any opening statements?

George: Yes, your honor. May it please the court, my name again is George Paul, representing the petitioner. The purpose of this hearing and the reason we are here today is that the personal representative declines to resign in favor of a neutral personal representative. We suggest that a neutral professional third party take over because of what has gone on, what is still going on, and what will continue to go on in the form of a dysfunctional administration of the estate. This relief is not very intrusive particularly because the testament trustee is to take over in any event to have a professional fiduciary coming on. What we are suggesting is that they come on a little bit earlier to alleviate what we say is dysfunctionality and other breach of duty.

So, a little about the facts. Raising teenagers is really never very easy. What we have in this case is a family who was raising three teenagers in the context of a dysfunctional marriage; this was Paul and Cindy Zimmermann and their three teenagers, Michelle, Kevin, and Joe. And the dysfunctional marriage turned into a divorce. Of course, that can't be easy either, and then of course the terrible tragedy that we will have to discuss a little bit is that right when the divorce was ending up, Mr. Paul Zimmermann suddenly disappeared. No one could find him. People mounted a search. He was gone for a week. The family was interrogated. The children were interrogated. And horribly, he was found brutally murdered by his business partner, his body in a plastic bag, his body decomposing in an empty lot in Scottsdale.

Now, needless to say, this is a horrific, traumatic, and a horrible thing for a family to go through. So that is kind of where our action picks up on this estate…this family now with Cindy, knowing that her children's father, the other parent, has been brutally murdered. How they are trying to pick up the pieces and trying to get together as a family and with three teenagers with some pre-existing issues.

All right, the very first thing that happened, after the funeral, after the children spread their father's ashes, they went up to the east coast and they visited the Zimmermanns, including Mark Zimmermann. When they came back, they were very upset. They were agitated, they were angry at their mother because their uncle had implied that their mother was going to try to steal their money.

He [Mark Zimmermann] had vowed to them, even though he would not get any kind of fiduciary, he had vowed to them, "I am not going to let them steal a dime of your money. I'm not going to let her steal a dime of your money." So, at least from her perspective we have a kind of triangulation thing going on here from the very beginning. The very beginning before he even gets appointed.

The next thing that happens, is he had been here for the funeral, he had been given a copy of Paul's will and a copy of Cindy's will for the purpose being to show that the estate plans were identical and the idea was to have the…trustee, to not give

A Woman of Interest

the kids the money all at once. You know, have an institutional trustee take things over.

And he starts calling and e-mailing people: Where's the original? Where's the original? Where's the original? Okay, he talked [to, and] e-mailed Diane Prescott, the attorney that was just excused. He e-mailed Cindy, and all of this came to a head on August 6, when he called up Cindy and said, "Where is the original, do you have the original will?" And she said, "Yes, I've got it."

And he said, "Whoa, things are going to be a lot easier without a will. I think it's better to go intestate. Because intestate we will get rid of this institutional trustee, they're expensive." Now, Mr. Zimmermann is a licensed member of the bar and practices law in Connecticut, and he knows exactly what he was suggesting here, frauding the court.

All right, but because of that legal office and that legal privilege he has, Cindy listened to him. This is her immediately former brother-in-law. So he says, "Look, well, you're going to have destroy the original will. Just pretend like you can't find it." So she temporarily decides, she is temporarily persuaded, that she is going to go along with this scheme of his and she writes an e-mail to him.

Sharon: Is this what the exhibit is?

George: Yes, yes, this is Exhibit 3. I'm pretty sure. Exhibit 3.

Sharon: Okay, thank you.

George: Your honor, we provided you photocopies of the exhibits…I think they are they are exhibit 3.

This is August 6 at 2:11 p.m. from Cindy to Mark:

"I have looked extensively and I am not able to find the original will." So she's playing her role here. So obviously something didn't sit right. She called her attorney, she called her sister, and she called a woman who works for the police named Natalie Summit to get counsel.

And they all said, "What are thinking, you cannot do this, this is unacceptable. No way…[Her attorney added] matter of fact, I will withdraw if you do something like this as your attorney." So she woke up the next morning and wrote the following e-mail: "I'm sorry, I can't say there is an original will or if there isn't. From what you said, it might have been easier with some shortcuts that are not worth being dishonest over and can turn out to be very long." And then she goes onto talk about the trustee, saying, "They're not that bad."

Is there some kind of e-mail [response], "What are you talking about, destroy the will, what are you sorry about?" The only [response] is to give the original to Sharon Moyer.

Okay, so the very first thing we have before he [Mark Zimmermann] even becomes a personal representative is contempt for his brother's estate plan. He's going to rewrite the whole estate plan, destroy the will, trick the court—and this didn't get things off to a real good start in the context of this family where the father of the kids had just been brutally murdered two weeks earlier.

Well, from that point forward we just have a succession of problems, a succession of issues.

Dysfunctionality, ill feelings, hostility. We've got Mr. Mark Zimmermann claiming that a check is forged, when Cindy knows it's not forged and she is unwilling to support that. There was an attempt to get back $22,000 dollars involving the purchase of a vehicle for a girlfriend.

We've got him changing Paul's bills into her name and sending his bills to her address. We've got a dispute over an IRA that lasts many months. And there are lawyers and lawyers and lawyers involved. It has ended up costing Cindy Zimmermann over 75,000 dollars that she just gives up.

Her allegation is that Mark drug his feet and refused to sign some papers for several months during this market collapse we had about a year ago and he has pointed several obligations against her.

And I don't know, your honor, who has to figure out who's right, who's wrong, who's good, who's bad. Everybody in this case will agree these people do not get along. It's like oil and water, cats and dogs. It's just like matter and anti-matter.

We've got a whole host of other incidents. There was a dispute as to whether Kevin, the gentleman who is going to testify on the phone, whether he should get to drive the truck of the man who murdered his father. Cindy did not want him driving the truck. Paul, before he had been murdered, had purchased the truck from the man who murdered him. And it was owned by the estate."

Judge: And what was his name?

George: Tom Sullivan.

So they get into a fight about this. "I don't want him driving the truck, he is not in the right mental state. I certainly do not want him driving a truck that was from the man who murdered his dad. And I protest." Mark said, "Well, he's going to drive the truck. I'm making it available to him." He's squelching her parental authority. She was having some problems with Kevin at the time—again, as a father of teenagers, I can sympathize. I think maybe we all can.

All right, but she did not own the truck; he was bigger than her. So what happened is that, yeah, he drove the truck, and guess what? He used it to commit criminal mischief; he got arrested. He got a criminal record. It's been expunged now. But oh, what a time-consuming and horrendous thing to do, yet more power struggles, more power play, triangulation.

Okay, we've got a continuing refusal to pay statutory allowances. Mr. Zimmermann made one payment. He said, "I don't like what you're doing with the money, I am cutting you off." Now this is to a woman whose mortgage payments are higher than her take-home pay and who was awarded $2,500 dollars a month for spousal maintenance from the divorce, which has now evaporated because of the murder. He doesn't like the way she is spending the money. No statutory allowances.

This has been going on for many months of dispute. He had written umpteen letters about statutory allowances. He refuses to pay for health insurance. It's right there in the divorce decree; it's enforceable continued obligations. This has been going on for months. Now whether intentional or not, this is the really, I think, subtle and sophisticated part of this case that really we suggest calls for a real vision of what a court of equity should be.

There is alienation going on—subtle and not so subtle. I don't know if it is intentional, I'm sure Mr. Zimmermann has been horribly traumatized by his brother's murder as well. But I'm not here to judge. I'm just saying what the facts are. He has implied to her kids that the mother is trying to steal from them.

She even got into a fight with the eldest son, Joe over [this]. "Mom, why didn't you just tear up the will? If Uncle Mark wanted you to tear up the will, that is what's best for us. Why didn't you just tear up the will?" So she's now been put in a position fighting with her children about basically defrauding the court, of having to justify why she refused to do that.

Other kinds of triangulations and alienation are [that] on one occasion Mark came into town and he got Kevin to swear to secrecy that they were meeting. Kevin lied to his mother and said he was going to visit his girlfriend. He wasn't visiting his girlfriend; he was off with Uncle Mark. This led to a very nasty fight, with my client losing her temper because she felt betrayed. And again who is the instigator? Uncle Mark the fiduciary. The guy that is supposed to be helping the family in the context of the brutal murder of his brother.

We've got him—and I'll try to speed up here—even after her objection, [Mark] e-mailing them, giving them reports, having them check up on her [about] what she and her attorney are up to? "Your mom is demanding everything, she is being unreasonable in some negotiations. You know we are going to have to go court and it's going to cost you a lot of money."

So, this isn't really making her life any easier, it's more like torturing her. Next we've got a complete impasse under the divorce decree. Before his murder, Paul swore and disclaimed any sole and separate property.

Sharon: Objection to the extent we are talking about statements by somebody who is deceased. Not admissible.

Judge: I don't think a dead man's statute would be applicable to an objection regarding that matter. I think that as it relates to pleadings in the related dissolution matter the court can always take a position in those.

George: My point is look, he is deceased. This is what he said before he died. I don't have any sole and separate properties. He was a generous man and you know they were getting divorced. I bet he had a place in his heart for her and vice versa, and that was the position he took. And this happens all the time in divorces, people give up a little sole and separate properties and that is what he decided to do. And then the divorce decree and the agreement, and they are splitting everything 50/50. It's very simple, 50/50—he doesn't have any separate property; they're splitting everything 50/50.

Now we've got when we [ask] where our 50 percent is. Mark Zimmermann says, "You're not getting 50 percent." He has come up with some new theories to challenge the divorce decree. "Ahhhh, my brother must have made a mistake when he said he didn't have any sole or separate property. I think that maybe he did, part of that pension is sole and separate property."

Well the problem is he is not doing anything about it. If he wants to challenge a very clear consent judgment, he's got to do so under Rule 60c. He's got a six-month deadline for fraud, mistakes, all that kind of stuff. That six months is over, long ago. So he is putting us to the expense of unnecessary litigation to enforce this divorce decree.

Needlessly, it's part of the same pattern of dysfunctionality. The destruction of the will, the bogus forged check, the divorce decree—there are several other things about the divorce decree that have been a problem, too. So again, without being judgmental, judge, this isn't working, this isn't working. We just want someone that's neutral and partial. We can work with them [and] if they want to take certain positions, we will deal with them.

Judge: Are you proposing any particular certified fiduciary?

George: Not at this point. I thought that would be a little bit ahead of the game, [but] this is little bit of 30 seconds of [my] closing argument. But it's very clear the court of equity has discretions with this. This is not in the best interest of the estate. We think these things are breaches of duty and we are thinking this is something very minimal for what

	we are asking: just get the professional in a little bit earlier, because they're coming in anyway. Thank you, your honor.
Judge:	Thank you. Counsel, any opening statements?
Sharon:	Yeah, Please. It seems like it's an easy fix here. Let's just get an independent fiduciary and kick Mark out. There are a few problems with that. First of all, the petitioner comes nowhere near to meeting the statutory requirements. This is what we really have got going on here. We've got Mark who is trying to preserve as much of the estate as possible for the three beneficiaries, the kids—none of whom, by the way, are here testifying today, even though, well Kevin will be here. But he's going to say he wants Mark to stay as the PR. The other two, Joe, who is over 18, and Michelle—how old is Michelle?
Mark:	14 or 15?
Sharon:	Those two are not going to be here. Those are the beneficiaries. What we have is the ex-wife, who is a creditor to the estate. Who is saying kick out the PR. You know why kick out the PR? Because he's not giving me all the money I want. He's making sure to preserve the estate for my kids. That's what's going on here.

So, we have Mark Zimmermann, who is trying to follow what the will says and try to make sure that the money needs to go [to who it's meant to go to], he feels an obligation.

So go back to why he just doesn't walk out.

Number One: because he feels an obligation to make sure the money goes where it's supposed to be. |

A Woman of Interest

Two: He was the alternative PR; he was named to be PR. His brother put him in the will to be PR. And he wants to be the PR. He hasn't violated any of the duties.

The third reason is, you know, yeah, he's a lawyer. Is he charging the estate anything for the hundreds, probably thousands, of hours he's spent? NO. What's a private fiduciary going to do? Charge. To go back and unravel that divorce decree that was entered a year ago and figure out who should get what?

And let Cindy Zimmermann now re-bring all these claims from the last year that she's been bringing for the last year? Mark has been analyzing [this] with counsel help. With third-party counsel help. To say, "Should I pay it, should I not? What's the right thing here?" So, this isn't as simple as whether Mark is just being mean to Cindy. Mark was just trying to do the right thing by the kids.

Cindy is trying to maximize how much money she gets out of her ex-husband's estate. She is a creditor. Her kids are the beneficiaries, the interested parties, and you won't hear one single one of them say, "Remove Uncle Mark."

You will hear Kevin say, "I trust Uncle Mark, Uncle Mark is doing the right thing. He's not said anything negative about her. She is the one trashing him and I want him to stay as PR to protect my interest. I don't want to pay a third-party fiduciary, he can do it."

He didn't ask her to destroy the will. When you see the e-mails, first of all, one of the things that is going to be a problem here is there is going to be a lot of hearsay, so we are going to have to cut through that. When you actually hear the admissible testimony, you're going to see that Mark comes to Phoenix to attend the funeral. Cindy gave him a copy of the will; this is true. He goes back to Connecticut and he follows up with her. July 30, sends her an e-mail saying "Hey, I need the original will." We don't have a response to that e-mail.

He then e-mails Diane Prescott on August 4 and says, "Hey, Cindy says you might have the original will." We don't have a response to that.

Then on August 6 we have an e-mail that says, "I can't find the original," and we have a follow-up e-mail that says, "I have the original and I can't say that it's not real."

Now this is what happened, they have a conversation...Mark and Cindy. And in that conversation they say okay, there has to be an original, otherwise it's going to be a hassle, will have to file for probate, blah blah blah. A copy of it doesn't do us much good. Paul didn't really do us many favors by not updating this thing because we have this out-of-state trust company that we don't even know exists anymore.

Then we don't know if she looked for the will at that point. We don't know, and then the will shows up. The original will shows up. Mark will testify that I never asked her to destroy the will. And really, when you think about, it why would he? He's not the beneficiary. What does he get out of a destroyed

A Woman of Interest

will? Absolutely nothing, so what's the incentive for him to do that?

There will unfortunately be a lot of testimony about did he pay this bill, did he refuse that bill.? Did he take this position, did he take that position?

The one thing I think that is the important thing to remember here is there a basis of removal. Let's take the QDRO [Qualified Domestic Relations Order] issue. Okay, there was a Caremark pension that was subject to distribution under the divorce decree. Because Paul died right, then Mark is unfortunately left in the wonderful position of divorcing his brother's ex-wife. Oh, fun. So he's got to look at the divorce decree and say, "What does this all mean?" The parties are supposed to hire a QDRO attorney. They hire...

Mark: Robert Harrian.

Sharon: Robert Harrian. Thank you. Robert Harrian looks at the situation and he says, "Geez, you guys, there's an issue here because...part of that Caremark pension was Paul's sole and separate. He had that Caremark pension before he married Cindy. So, you know this is an issue." So Mark consults with Paul's divorce attorney, Chuck Hallam. Chuck says, "Well, geez, you guys, you know it's only ever contemplated that you're gonna split up the community property portion of this kind of stuff. And that's what was contemplated by the divorce decree."

Okay, so now we have an issue, all right...Mark's position, based on what Paul's lawyer says, is you can only divide the community property portion of that Caremark pension. Cindy's position is, "No, no, no, no, no, it's all of it, it's all of it—even the sole and separate.

So what happens with that? Well, you probably don't remember this, but when we were back here, right when this petition was filed, several months ago, we were talking about okay, how we have a petition for removal, plus we have a petition to help us figure out what to do with this divorce decree because now it's sort of a probate matter, isn't it? How are we going to divide this up? What's going to go in the estate? What's going to go to Cindy? What's ultimately going to funnel to the trust? And we talked about, "Will this have to go back to the divorce court?" No, this court has jurisdiction. So, this isn't as if Mark hasn't been doing anything about this. This petition is before you.

He doesn't know how to divide it. He's got a lawyer saying, "Hey, you know there's an issue, and now you're just going to give the money to Cindy and you're going to give a breach of fiduciary claim to the kids. No, you're going to ask the courts guidance. Now it came at this instant through Mr. Paul filing the petition. Okay, fine.

You know, Mark was trying to settle for the settle petition that comes to you that way. It doesn't really make a difference how the issue comes to you. But it's agreed by Mark that he can't make the decision on his own on the QDRO because of this issue. You'll also hear about an 11,000-dollar joint Schwab joint account that there's a dispute about. He's saying, "I can't just distribute this because there is a dispute, and I'm going to be giving the kids a breach of fiduciary duty plan if I just pay this money out, so let's let the court decide.

We have issues about alienation of the children, interesting because I don't know how Mrs. Zimmermann is going to prove…I mean, her kids aren't here to testify about what Mark said to them. So I think that's a non-issue. The only one that is going to be here to testify is going to say, "You know what? Any alienation that occurred has occurred as a result of my interaction with my mom, and my mother, for example, blaming me for the divorce and my mother blaming me for the death of my father, that was enough to alienate me from my mother and get me to hightail it out of Phoenix as fast as I could and move to Colorado."

I want to make sure that one legal issue is made clear. I don't think that Ms. Zimmermann can act on behalf of her daughter…I say that because if you look at 1406, if you look at a parent's ability to represent the interest of a minor child, she's only got Michelle now at home. Where she can't act for Joe or Kevin, they are their own entities and they can move; they can ask to remove Mark on their own and they are not doing that. Theoretically, she could move and represent Michelle. We don't know that, and Michelle isn't saying that, and in fact Cindy's position of "I want more in my own pocket" is directly contradictory to the position of the kids.

Every penny in her pocket is a penny out of the kids'. So my position is that under 14-1406 there is language…there is a material conflict of interest between Ms. Zimmermann and Michelle Zimmermann, and I don't think she can move as the Mom of a beneficiary. Her only basis, then, to bring this petition is as a creditor. And so what we've got here is a fairly interesting issue, we've got a creditor on the one hand who's saying kick him out because he's not paying me what I think I'm due, and then we have a beneficiary, Kevin, who is willing to testify, and say keep Uncle Mark, he's acting in the best interest of the estate. And I think that is the issue that we've got.

Judge: Thank you very much; you may call your first witness.

George: Cindy Zimmermann, your honor.

Judge: Please step forward ma'am. As you walk forward, I just ask you approach the clerk and she will swear you in for the purposes of these proceedings, and will you raise your right hand please.

(Swearing in)

Judge: Okay, thank you. You may proceed.

George: Thank you. State your name, please.

Cindy: Cindy Zimmermann.

George: And are you related to the three beneficiaries of this estate?

Cindy: Yes, I am. I am Joe and Kevin and Michelle Zimmermann's mother.

George: Now, without going into too much detail, could you please just go briefly go into the chronology of the divorce proceedings and your ex-husband's death?

Cindy: I was married to Paul for 23 years. The last couple of years of our marriage were very dysfunctional, and we mutually sought a divorce. [We] started out with the intentions of having a collaborative divorce. It became very tumultuous very quickly. So we had to hire separate lawyers. We spent a year and half, approximately, working through negotiations. Finally came to a settlement. Finally worked out our assets and towards the very end of that, on a weekend, Paul became missing. And… um *(crying)*…he was murdered. And it's been very difficult for my children it was very difficult at the time; he was missing for two days. We didn't know where he was.

Judge: I'm sorry—did you say two days?

Cindy: I don't remember exactly, it was about maybe two days…we didn't know exactly where he was. And so we had hoped he was just missing. Unfortunately, my children had to be involved in the police investigation. They had to be interrogated. They had to identify pictures; it was just this unraveling of…and eventually we had to hear all of the gory details. We were advised by the police to [stay put] in Paul's home because the media was interviewing us as we would go in and out of the house. We had to keep the shades down in the house, so the kids were under—and I was under—a great deal of just awfulness. And so then the police found what had happened to him…that he was murdered by his business partner. And I wasn't certain if our divorce was done. I didn't really know what was going on. I called Steve Smith, my divorce attorney, to find out if our divorce was done. He had to call the judge to find out if our divorce was even done. As it turns out, our divorce was actually signed the same day Paul was murdered.

George: Now I assume this was very difficult on the children.

Cindy: It was very difficult for them. They loved their father very much. It is heartbreaking.

George: All right. Now, I assume there was a funeral, here in Phoenix, or a service?

Cindy: Yes, there was.

George: Did the children go up to visit the Zimmermann family, including Mark, after the funeral?

Cindy: Yes they did. They traveled with their father's ashes to Florida to bury the ashes in Paul's parents' golf community in Florida. The Zimmermann family had asked if they could have the kids for a while in Connecticut. So, I said yes, that they could go there for a week.

George: And when they came back to town, what was their state of mind?

Cindy: They were really, really, upset.

Judge: I hate to interrupt, but when you say kids, are you referring to all three of the children?

Cindy: Yes, all three kids.

Judge: Okay.

George: What were they upset at?

Cindy: They were upset because Mark had said...

Sharon: Objection. Hearsay.

George: Your honor…I prepared a bench memo on this, and I would like to be heard on it.

Judge: Sure.

George: The state of mind of the beneficiaries and the interested parties, which are also the fiduciary duties, which is directly relevant in this case as an independent evidentiary fact. And it's not being offered to prove the truth of the matter for certain. It's been offered to show that the children were upset, and they were upset by Mark Zimmermann. For example, if Mark…says to them that your mom is trying to steal all your money…if we bring them on to say that, we are not obviously trying to prove that [their] mother is trying to steal all their money. We are trying to prove that he said that, that upset them, and that agitated them. So it goes to the state of mind, and is defined as not hearsay because it's not being offered to prove the truth of the matter observed.

Sharon: Your honor, the kids' state of mind has absolutely nothing to do with this. The question is, did Mark say something so as to alienate the children from their mother? The whole issue is whether there was a statement made. The best evidence of that is going to be from Mark or from the children.

Judge: I'm ready to rule. I don't find it to be hearsay under the circumstances presented; it's not being offered to prove the truth of the matter asserted, so I'll allow it. And then other concerns that you have regarding those statements coming in really goes to weight rather than the admissibility. So you may re-ask your question, counsel.

George: Thank you. Just to recap, when they came back they were upset. Okay, what were they upset at?

Cindy: They were upset because they were worried about their finances. Kevin was worried about the payments for his truck. The kids were worried because Mark had told them that he would make sure I wouldn't get one single penny from the estate. And I wouldn't be able to steal anything from them. They were literally crying in my arms. They were very, very upset about how this estate was going to play out. I immediately called Natalie Summit.

George: Who is that?

Cindy: She is the police advocate that was assigned to our family who was to give me guidance on counselors, resources in the community, grief support groups, the New Song Grief Support Center. I was asking for help on what should I do. She had advised me...

Sharon: Objection. Hearsay.

Judge: You can talk generally, but not specific words that you want us to know. You can say what the general advice was.

Cindy: Okay.

George: Why don't we start going more in summary, because we have a lot to cover. Natalie Summit advised you, why don't we just skip over that. Okay?

Cindy: Okay.

George: All right, so you tried to cope with the situation. Is that what happened?

Cindy: Yes.

George: Okay. Now turning to this issue of the will, did there come a time when Mark started asking you questions about where the original was will?

Cindy: Yes he did, and I was surprised because when he was out for the funeral I gave him a copy of Paul's will and I gave him a copy of my will. I volunteered that to him. I wanted him to see that Paul and I had the same wishes. And I was trying to work with him. So I really couldn't understand why he was pressuring me and kept asking me about the original will. I was really, really busy. I had to get the kids back into school. Kevin was moving into my house. I had to get a storage unit because I didn't have room for his things. I was again trying to find counseling for the kids. There was a stolen identity. The man that murdered Paul had all of our financial records. So I was trying to protect checking accounts. I had a lot to do.

George: But he was insistent that you tell him about the original will?

Cindy: Yes, I felt like I had already given him that information. So I didn't really understand why that kept coming up.

George: Did you refer him to anyone?

Cindy: I told him to talk to Diane. Diane Prescott was my attorney.

George: Okay, now did you ever have a phone conversation with him about this will?

Cindy: Yes, I did.

George: When was that?

Cindy: August 6.

Judge: And what year? I'm sorry, ma'am?

Cindy: 2008.

George: Okay, as best as you can remember, can you recount that phone conversation, please?

Cindy: I remember it very clearly. I was standing in my bedroom. I was looking out the window. I was right by a chair. And he was talking to me about this original will and how it would make things much easier if there wasn't a trust involved. And...

George: Let me stop you here. Did he ask you whether you had found the original will?

Cindy: He asked me if I *had* the original will.

George: If you *had* the original will.

Cindy: Yes.

George: And what did you say?

Cindy: I said yes.

George: Okay, go ahead.

Cindy: And he said it would be much easier if there was not a trust involved. That trusts are really expensive. He could do it much cheaper. It would become intestate and would I destroy the will?

George: Okay, and what did you say?

Cindy: I said that yes, I would.

George: And why did you say that?

Cindy: Because he had been my brother-in-law. He's an attorney. I thought that he knew best. There had

A Woman of Interest

been so much confusion about am I divorced, not divorced, who's the personal representative. My oldest son Joe…there was some question about whether he would be the personal representative. I mean, there was just a lot going on. So I assumed that Mark would know best.

George: Okay, and after you hung up, did you write him an e-mail?

Cindy: Yes I did.

George: Okay, Referring your attention to Exhibit 3…. What is this writing down here at the bottom?

Cindy: That's the e-mail that I sent to Mark; that I was part of the plan that he asked me to do.

George: Is that a true and correct copy of your e-mail?

Cindy: Yes, it is.

George: Okay, move it to admission, your honor.

Judge: Any objection?

Sharon: No objection.

Judge: Exhibit 3 will be admitted.

George: Okay, so that's from you to Mark, Wednesday at 2:11, at least in Phoenix, presumably.

Cindy: That's correct.

George: What did you say?

Cindy: I had looked extensively and I am not able to find the original will.

George: Why did you say that?

Cindy: Because he asked me to destroy the will. So that we could have this intestate type estate without a trust involved.

George: Okay, and you were kind of playing along? Is that right?

Cindy: Yes. I was.

George: Now after you wrote that, did you begin having second thoughts?

Cindy: I did. I started thinking about shredding documents, legal documents, so I called Diane Prescott, my attorney, and I called my sister and told them about the conversation, and I called Natalie Summit, the police advocate.

George: Okay, what did you tell them?

Cindy: I told them about the conversation and I told them about the e-mail.

George: Now let me ask you this. Could you have been having some conversations with Mark Zimmermann where you kind of misinterpreted what he was saying?

Cindy: No, I did not misunderstand what he said.

George: Are you sure that he was asking you to destroy the original [will] of your ex-husband?

Cindy: I am absolutely certain that he was asking me to be part of this plan of there not being an original will. So that there would not be a trust involved in this estate.

George: Alright, now you mentioned your attorney Diane Prescott, who is here out in the hall. What did you say to her?

Cindy: I told her about our conversation. And that I was going to be tearing up this will.

George: And what did she say?

Sharon: Objection. Hearsay.

George: Your honor, I think there's been an implication that this testimony about the destruction of the will is exaggerated or has changed because of an improper motive. This is what was said about this conversation that very day, this part of our trial brief, that's Section 1 of the trial brief. This is a prior consistency statement of [Cindy] to Diane and they are discussing this whole thing about what to do.

Sharon: Ms. Zimmermann already testified about what she said to Diane. Now they want to…

Judge: I'm going to await the testimony from Ms. Prescott prior to ruling on that issue.

George: Okay, without saying what she said, she gave you certain advice.

Cindy: Yes she did. Very clear advice.

George: And as a result of that advice, did you change your attitude about whether you should go along with this whole concept?

Cindy: Yes, I did.

George: What was your new thinking after talking to your attorney?

Cindy: That I was absolutely not going to be tearing up legal documents and be a part of Mark's plan.

George: And what did you do?

Cindy: The next morning I got up and I wrote Mark an e-mail first thing in the morning. I said, "I'm sorry I couldn't say there wasn't an original will when there is one. From what you said it might have been easier, but some shortcuts aren't worth being dishonest over and can turn out to be very expensive and very long. I looked up First of America Bank Trust on the web and recalled how we chose them. They were very well respected back in the 90s. I guess there are worse places to end up as far as trusts go."

George: And this is a true and correct copy of your e-mail? I think it's already in evidence. It's part of the same exhibit, Exhibit 3.

Cindy: Yes, it is.

George: So did Mark e-mail you back and say what are you talking about?

Cindy: No.

George: What did he do?

Cindy: He sent me an e-mail later in the day that said, "Take the original will over to Sharon Moyer."

George: Sharon Moyer was his attorney at the time?

Cindy: I assume so. Yes.

George: Have you filed a bar complaint?

Cindy: Yes, I have.

George: Okay. Now let's talk about some of the problems. Was there anything other than this suggestion that the will be destroyed that has happened in your interactions with Mark?

Cindy: Yes. One of the first things that happened was…he wanted to take the position that one of the checks with Chase Bank was a forged check for $22,000. In an e-mail to me, he said, "Just want you to know I'm taking the position that these two checks were forged." I had clearly told him that check wasn't forged. He knew that it wasn't forged. He knew that Paul wrote that check to pay for…

Sharon: Objection, your honor. I don't know, I mean this allegation has never been set forth in any petition whatsoever. And I don't know where the e-mails are, and we just had a deposition and I never heard about this, so I don't know what we have here.

Judge: Okay, well you can point out any questions that you have in cross-examination.

George: Go ahead, finish.

Cindy: I told him I'm not going to go along with any forgeries, in particular with a bank. You can tell its Paul's signature. We already talked about the car, because this person was at the funeral. And we were all…

George: Okay, we will be here all day if we go into too much detail over each of these incidences. But there was a dispute over whether he was legitimately claiming a check was a forgery—is that a fair summary?

Cindy: That is correct.

George: Okay, now was there anything else? Like involving cell phone bills?

Cindy: Yes, cell phone bills. He started changing them into my name. They were Paul's bills. I got a letter from Verizon that said Mark called and told us to change...

Sharon: Objection. If we have a document let's have it, it sounds like hearsay to me.

Judge: Sustained.

George: What was the dispute, without telling us what Verizon said?

Cindy: He wanted me to pay the bills that were in Paul's name that were the estate's responsibility. I could not believe he could change bills into my name.

George: Did you ultimately end up having to pay the bills?

Cindy: Yes. He deducted them out of the first and only support check. Whatever you call it?

George: Statutory allowance?

Cindy: Yes, sir.

George: Were there any problems involving the truck with Kevin?

Cindy: Yes. He [Mark] immediately wanted me to start paying for the truck insurance for Kevin. I told him the truck is part of the estate, and I was not responsible for paying for it. I didn't even want Kevin to drive the truck. I was very clear about that from the beginning. I did not want Kevin to drive the truck from the man that killed his father. I thought it was psychologically just sick, and we had many disagreements about it. But I couldn't do anything because the truck was not in my name.

A Woman of Interest

George: So you had many disagreements with Mark about whether Kevin should drive this truck, sold to your ex by the man that murdered him?

Cindy: My ex bought it from the man that murdered him.

George: What happened with that truck dispute?

Cindy: It went on and on. I had interactions with the insurance company. Letting them know that I had been advised that it was a risk to the estate to have Kevin driving it. Because had he been in a car accident, the estate would...

Sharon: Objection. Hearsay.

Judge: This isn't really offered for the truth of the matter, sort of...just to provide that she took the steps that she did. So I'll allow you to continue, ma'am.

Cindy: My children's estate was at risk because had Kevin been in a car accident somebody could have sued the estate by him driving it. Also I could not parent him because I did not have my name on the title. I had called Natalie Summit again and said, "I can't have Kevin come in at curfew because he does whatever he wants to with this truck. Can I get a boot on it? Can I put it in an impound? What can I do?" I could do nothing—I would have been arrested had I done anything with that truck, because it is not in my name. I talked to police officers about it.

George: Did Mark know that you were objecting to this?

Cindy: Yes, he did.

George: And he was providing the truck to Kevin, your minor son, over your objections?

Cindy: Yes, he was.

George: And what happened with the truck?

Cindy: Well, eventually I thought the insurance will run out, it was about the end of December. And I thought maybe if it's not insured any more that I can get rid of it in that fashion. Unfortunately, one night Kevin destroyed public property with it. I was called at midnight I was and had to go pick him up when he was arrested.

Judge: What does that mean, Kevin destroyed public property with it?

Cindy: He took the truck with some other young man in the car and tore up baseball fields on city property.

Judge: What city?

Cindy: Scottsdale Ranch Park baseball fields.

Judge: Okay. Thank you.

George: Did that get him in trouble with the law?

Cindy: Yes, it did.

George: That was the result of this truck, the fact that he had access to the truck over your objections?

Cindy: Yes it [was]. And that night I told the police officer this truck will not leave this parking lot. I have been trying to get rid of this truck for six months. And I said, "Please call Mark Zimmermann right now and tell him to do whatever he needs to do to get of this truck." The police called him…

Sharon: Objection. Hearsay.

Judge: Sustained.

A Woman of Interest

George: Why don't we just move on? Did you have any problem involving health insurance?

Cindy: Yes I did. Within the first week Mark started pressuring me on "you need to start taking care of this health insurance. I need to discontinue paying it and you need to find health insurance for the kids and yourself."

George: Have you since then pointed out to him that the divorce decree requires Paul to pay for half of the health insurance?

Cindy: Yes. I have.

George: And has he agreed to pay for half the health insurance?

Cindy: No.

George: And is it a continuing dispute, the health insurance?

Cindy: Yes, it is.

George: How long has that been going on?

Cindy: From the very beginning, five days after the funeral.

George: All right. Now did you have a dispute involving some sort of financial fund called Ameriprise, the Ameriprise IRA?

Cindy: Yes, we did.

George: How long did that dispute go on?

Cindy: Six months.

George: Okay, just very, very briefly summarize if you will what the dispute was?

Cindy: In the divorce decree I was assigned approximately $93,000 that supposed to be transferred within ten days of the divorce decree. And because of Paul's death it was difficult to get that transaction done. Also because of the market, it was plummeting at that time. So there was a lot of angst in the financial markets. I called Ameriprise. I tried a number of times to get the transfer made. I was not able to do it; one reason was because they wanted to make sure that I was not a suspect in the murder. I had to get a letter from the police, which I did. I faxed that over immediately to them in August. I again asked for my $93,000. Mark put a block on my Ameriprise and said, "No, this money is not hers." There's always a long-going dispute whether it was $93,000 or whether it was affected by the market fluctuations. So as the time went on, the amount became less and less because of the declining financial markets.

George: And have you accepted a lesser amount? Basically giving in to Mark's position?

Cindy: Yes, I did.

Judge: I'm sorry, what was that lesser amount? If you recall?

Cindy: I gave up approximately 75,000 dollars.

George: And your position—and again I know there [are] two positions—your position is that he just refused to release the money and the delay during the financial chaos basically destroyed the value of the investment.

Cindy: That's correct.

George: Okay. And then he has his position; I suppose he'll say it…It lasted about six months and involved four or five lawyers?

Cindy: That's correct.

George: Now has Mark been paying you the statutory allowances?

Cindy: No.

George: Did he pay one payment?

Cindy: Yes, he did.

George: Then what happened?

Cindy: He didn't like it because he didn't like the way I was spending the money. I had told him in an e-mail that I would be opening a bank account because I wanted it to be very, very forthcoming that he could be able to see exactly how I was spending the money. And for some reason he took that to mean that I was using it as savings. But it was my attempt to try to be very transparent with how I was spending any of this money that is for my children.

George: And is there an ongoing dispute over the statutory allowances?

Cindy: Yes, there is.

George: He's refused to pay you more than that first payment?

Cindy: That's correct.

George: Now at any point, because of advice you received, did you just stop talking to him?

Cindy: Yes, I did.

George: And did you ask him to talk to your attorneys instead?

Cindy: That's correct.

George: And did he honor that request?

Cindy: No, he did not.

George: Now I see that Mark is calling your son Kevin to testify here. Have you sought to involve your children in these matters?

Cindy: No, I haven't.

George: Have you tried to keep them out of this?"

Cindy: Yes, I have.

George: Okay. Why aren't you having all of your kids come and testify for you?

Cindy: Because I think that it is unconscionable.

George: You just don't think that they should have to suffer through that stress?

Cindy: No, I don't. I wanted my children to be able to go on and live their lives. I've sent this to Mark in a number of e-mails. "Please quit sending information about these things to the kids. Please let them go on and live their lives." I want them to be able to try to emotionally get over the loss of their dad and also the tremendous standard of living adjustment.

George: Okay, let's talk just a little bit more about the kids. Before…Paul's murder, did you have some issues with Kevin?

Cindy: Yes.

George: What kind of issues?

Cindy: Kevin did not want to live with me; he wanted to live with his father full time.

George: Did he have a different lifestyle over there?

Cindy: Yes, he did.

George: And what was the difference?

Cindy: He had a credit card that he could use at his will. Paul bought the truck for him. He was able to run wild and just do whatever he wanted to do without supervision.

George: Okay. Now did you have basically some of the issues that people have with teenagers during the last part of the marriage?

Cindy: Yes.

George: And how about during the divorce?

Cindy: Yes, we did.

George: And did they get better or worse after your ex-husband's murder?

Cindy: There [were] a lot of…things through the divorce because the children were so affected by the divorce, and I would say the last six months or nine months, we would make a little progress, and then Mark would get involved in some way and we'd take a couple steps back. But I'm very proud of my children and they are, I think, working through their grief.

George: Now, focusing on the kids' state of mind and your state of mind. Has Mark made things better or worse after he took over as personal representative?

Cindy: He makes things worse.

George: How does he do that?

Cindy: It's like pouring gasoline on a fire, and if he hears that
            there is a problem in my house, rather than maybe
            extending a hand to me and saying, "Cindy, what
            can I do to help," it's more saying to the kids…

Sharon: Objection. Hearsay.

George: State of mind, your honor.

Judge: You may answer.

Cindy: Your mom drinks too much, she loses her temper,
            she says inappropriate things to you…just…

George: Have you noticed any particular behaviors or con-
            duct that you feel causes ill feelings, agitation among
            the kids, among the beneficiaries?

Cindy: Yes, he is on a constant theme about how I am
            trying to steal money from them. He uses Kevin,
            in particular, to spy on me.

George: When you say spy on you, what are you talking
            about?

Cindy: He'll e-mail him and say, "Kevin, how did your
            Mom react…"

Sharon: Objection. Hearsay. Where's the e-mail?

George: One of your exhibits.

Judge: Refresh the question.

George: Okay. How do you know that he does this?

Cindy: Because you've submitted a copy of the e-mails to
            the court.

George: Right. Okay, what else has he done that you think
            is not conducive to good behavior in the family,

good feelings in the family, good feelings among the beneficiaries?

Cindy: Well, I mentioned to you earlier when he came out for the estate sale, he was very secretive about it. Secretive about when he was going to be seeing the kids.

George: Why was he keeping it a secret?

Cindy: I don't know...I didn't even know the exact dates of the estate sale. I had actually a pool guy call me that morning and say, "Cindy, did...

Sharon: Objection. Hearsay.

Judge: Overruled. You may continue.

Cindy: I had the pool guy...[who] had been our pool man for ten years, call me and say, "Cindy, I'm sorry to tell you this, but did you know that the children's bikes are in the front yard of Paul's house? They're selling them at the estate sale? And I said, "No, I did not know the estate sale was today.

George: Did he accuse any of your family members of stealing from the estate sale?

Cindy: Yes, he did. He accused my sister of stealing.

Sharon: Objection. Hearsay.

Judge: Sustained.

George: Okay. Is that your understanding?

Sharon: Objection. Hearsay.

Judge: The answer will stand.

George: All right now, if you ever have a disagreement with him, does he sometimes communicate that to the kids and indicate that it's going to cost them money?

Cindy: Yes, he has sent them many e-mails saying that I'm sorry...

Sharon: Objection. Hearsay. Do you have the e-mails?

George: Is this something that you learned from the children?

Sharon: Objection. Hearsay.

Judge: Are you objecting to the general concept that disputes costs money? Or that it was somehow communicated in e-mails?

Sharon: I'm objecting to, number one, that it's a communication that should come from either Mark or from the children, not secondhand. And secondly, that if there is essentially best evidence if we have a piece of paper that reflects that, then let's look at it.

Judge: Well, best evidence I don't think isn't an up-to-date kind of objection, but nonetheless, I will defer ruling on the objection and will allow counsel to question Mark Zimmermann regarding those matters.

George: All right.

Judge: And then, if necessary, this witness can always be recalled in rebuttal.

George: Now, personally, how have you been getting along with Mark in e-mail correspondence and otherwise?

Cindy: I haven't really had much correspondence with him since I think November of last year. Minimal.

George: And your e-mails before then...were they pleasant?

Cindy: I tried to be pleasant in them.

George: And how about his e-mails to you?

Cindy: He was threatening me and tried to use his power as an attorney to intimidate me and threaten me. And I believe in one e-mail that we've submitted, he said, "I will use my skills as an attorney." I can't remember, but we do have a copy of it that we submitted to the court.

George: Okay. Now when you asked to split the Caremark pension, which is part of the divorce decree. Paragraph 7, I think that is Exhibit 8. The decree of dissolution of marriage. Have you requested your half of that pension fund?

Cindy: Yes, I have.

George: And what is Mark's response?

Cindy: I was advised by you and Mark that I was supposed to write a check for a thousand dollars to this QDRO lawyer and he would take care of it, and it would be done. And I believe I got a phone call from you a few weeks later saying that all of a sudden this guy is calling you, telling you that there's a problem, and you were upset.

George: Well, don't talk about what you and I were talking about.

Cindy: Okay.

George: But what is Mark's position in your understanding?

Cindy: Now, all of a sudden, I don't get 50 percent.

George: Okay, and is that true of another fund as well?

Cindy: It's true—on the Schwab joint account, again I don't get 50 percent of that either.

George: What's the claim there?

Cindy: That I stole $11,000 from the account.

George: And did you steal $11,000 from the account?

Cindy: No, I did not.

George: All right. How did you have the authority to write checks on that account?

Cindy: Paul told me to write the checks.

Sharon: Objection. Your honor, dead man's statute 12—whatever it is.

Judge: Overruled. The answer will stand.

George: Has it been time-consuming dealing with Mark?

Cindy: Very time-consuming.

George: How time-consuming?

Cindy: In the beginning, I was getting e-mails from him in the morning almost daily, trying to work with him trying to get through the massive amounts of paperwork and fraud identity—all the things that needed to get done. I tried to work with him to the best of my ability.

George: Can you just briefly summarize your desire to have an independent neutral fiduciary appointed here? Why do you want that?

Cindy: Because I want to get on with my life with my children. And I want my children's lives to get on…throughout this whole process, if I give Mark an answer, it turns into an argument. Always. It's never, "Oh, okay"—everything is an argument; everything is put in a light that I am trying to steal money from my children. Any money that I have is my children's money. I don't understand where that line of thinking comes from. Last night, I'm out buying a homecoming dress for my daughter. I spend money on my children. As soon as Kevin's car was gone, I bought another car for Kevin. It's a 1,200-dollar car. I'm trying to pay the health insurance. I've been taking all this money out of savings, trying to keep my family together. So I don't understand. There are not any new yachts at my house...I just don't understand why someone would assume that money that I have I would not spend on my children. It is their money, either side of the fence, it's their money.

George: No further questions...your honor.

Judge: Any cross-examination?

Sharon: Yes, please.

Judge: You may proceed.

Sharon: You filed a bar complaint against Mark Zimmermann in September of 2009, is that right? About a week ago.

Cindy: Yes.

Sharon: And that was, I don't know, well over a year after he supposedly told you to destroy the will, right?

Cindy: Yes, that is correct.

Sharon: Did you file that so you that could tell the court that you filed a bar complaint today?

Cindy: No.

Sharon: You indicated that you haven't communicated with Mark since November of 2008, is that right?

Cindy: I believe I said that I've communicated with him minimally.

Sharon: Okay, how is it then that it has taken so much of your time to communicate with him?

Cindy: I believe I was talking about when he was first interacting with me, I was getting e-mails from him almost every morning trying to get through the process.

Sharon: And initially those were pretty friendly e-mails, weren't they?

Cindy: Yes.

Sharon: Now you are here as a creditor of the estate. Is that right?

Cindy: I am here for the interest of my children.

Sharon: Are you here as a creditor of the estate?

Cindy: I am also a creditor of the estate.

Sharon: You're not here on behalf of Kevin, right?

Cindy: In my heart, I am.

Sharon: Well, he's over 18…he's an adult, and you're not acting in his interest, are you?

Cindy: I will be acting in his interest as long as I am on the planet.

Sharon: You have the authority to act here and bring this petition.

Cindy: I don't know what that means.

Sharon: Did he say to you, "Mom, I want you to move to…I want you to file a petition to remove Uncle Mark as PR?

Cindy: As I mentioned to you, I do not talk to my children about these things extensively.

Sharon: So he didn't say that to you.

Cindy: We did not have a discussion about this.

Sharon: Okay, we don't know what Michelle's opinion is because she's not here to testify, right?

Cindy: That is correct, and I don't talk to her about this.

Sharon: And Joe Zimmermann is not here to testify.

Cindy: That is correct.

Sharon: So you're the only interested party asking for Mark's removal, right?

Cindy: To the best of my knowledge.

Sharon: Let me give you what's been marked. Let's see, we've got Exhibit 1 and we've got Exhibit 13. Can you take a look at those please and see if you identify them?…Let's look at 13 first, if you would, please. Do you recognize the document?

Cindy: Yes.

Sharon: What is it?

Cindy: It's an e-mail from Mark.

Sharon: To?

Cindy: To me.

Sharon: Okay, now you see that Mark is saying to you in this exhibit, "Cindy, the will you gave me last week is a copy." This is dated July 30, so is he referring to a will you gave him when he was here in Phoenix for the funeral?

Cindy: That is correct.

Sharon: And he says, "Do you have the original? We need an original to submit to probate court." Right?

Cindy: That was the beginning, when he started asking me about the original.

Sharon: Okay. You found something offensive about him asking for the original will?

Cindy: No.

Sharon: Did you have an understanding that he needed the original, because otherwise it was more of a hassle in probate court?

Cindy: Not in this e-mail.

Sharon: Okay, so you developed that understanding at some point.

Cindy: In a phone call with him.

Sharon: That the original, having the original, was important.

Cindy: I don't understand your question.

Sharon: Did you develop an understanding at some point that having the original will was important?

Cindy: I became…as things…

Sharon: It's really just a yes or a no.

George: Well, she can't just cut off the answers; it's not really just a yes or no question.

Sharon: It was really framed as a yes or no question.

George: She can't just cut off an answer she doesn't like, your honor.

Sharon: Did you at some point develop an understanding that having the original will was important? It's really a yes or no.

George: Well, I object.

Judge: And you can follow up and redirect.

George: Okay. Well, I object to telling a witness that they have to answer yes or no, because that's often very unfair; lawyers are experts at asking ambiguous questions.

Judge: Well, I am well aware of that, but you can answer it yes or no if you're able to do so.

Cindy: Can you ask me one more time, please?

Sharon: Sure. Did you develop an understanding at some point that having the original will was important?

Cindy: Yes. When I talked to Diane Prescott on the phone about it.

Sharon: No, no, no…Now your testimony at your deposition was that Mark knew that you had the original from the time he was here in Phoenix. Isn't that right?

Cindy: I don't recall.

Sharon: Okay…I have the…do you have a copy of the e-tran? Did I give you a copy of the e-tran? I did not mark it as an exhibit. The transcript of her deposition.

Judge: No, I did not receive a copy of that, you can certainly utilize that.

Sharon: Okay, so here is a copy of your deposition that was taken on September 30th 2009. And if you turn to page 9, you will see, looking at line 18…[it] says Question: So at the time that you were speaking with Mark you had found the original. Answer: I always had the original will and he knew that. Do you see that?

Cindy: Yes.

Sharon: So that was your testimony a couple of days ago, right?

Cindy: Yes.

Sharon: So then he knew before he sent you this July 30 e-mail saying, "Hey, do you have the original," he already knew you had the original. Is that your testimony?

Cindy: He knew there was an original.

Sharon: Did he know YOU had the original?

Cindy: Well, there was a bit of confusion about it because…

Sharon: No, no, no—did he know that you had the original?

Cindy: There was confusion.

Sharon: He didn't know. So your testimony at the depo the other day is inaccurate?

George: Objection, form compound.

Judge: Sustained.

Sharon: You testified at your deposition that Mark always knew you had the original will. Right? Was that your testimony at your deposition?

Cindy: Well, I'm only looking at one portion of this.

Sharon: Right.

Cindy: I haven't read the whole deposition, so I'm not sure if you ask me in another place if maybe I'm perjuring myself, and I'm not going to do that. I'm trying to be as honest with you as I can.

Sharon: Okay, this was your sworn testimony on September 30, right?

Cindy: This is one sentence of it.

Sharon: Right, and in that sentence and question and answer it indicates, "Yes, Mark always knew I had the original will." Right? That's what it says there.

Cindy: Okay.

Sharon: Is it?

Cindy: That is what it says.

Sharon: Okay. But yet on July 30 he's e-mailing you and saying, "Do you have the original will?" Right?

Cindy: Correct.

Sharon: And then if you take a look at…Exhibit 1, which you have in front of you there…he e-mails Diane Prescott on August 4 saying, "Cindy mentioned that you might have Paul's original 1992 will. Do you? Please let me know." Do you see that?

Cindy: Yes, I do.

Sharon: He already knew that you had the original. Is that your testimony when he sent this e-mail to Diane Prescott?

Cindy: My testimony is that there was confusion about this.

Sharon: Okay. Your e-mail, Exhibit 3. This one right here. Not true, right? That was a lie when you sent it?

Cindy: That's correct.

Sharon: And you knew it wasn't accurate when you sent it, right?

Cindy: Yes, I did.

Sharon: Knew you were lying?

Cindy: Yes, I was.

Sharon: Now, let's take a look at this other part of Exhibit 3. You say, "I'm sorry I couldn't say there wasn't an original will when there is one." Do you see anything in this e-mail that says I'm not going to destroy the will? Does it say anything about destroying a will?

Cindy: No.

Sharon: What's your understanding of what would have happened if we had only the original will and… we had only a copy of the will? What do you have an understanding of what would have happened? What would have happened?

Cindy: I didn't really know. All I know was that I was asked to destroy a legal document.

Sharon: Okay. Do you know that if we had only a copy, we would have still had a trust? Do you understand that?

A Woman of Interest

Cindy:	No, I don't know about that. I'm not an attorney.
Judge:	The answer will stand.
Sharon:	Well, let's assume for a moment…can you assume that for me? What would have been the benefit to Mark in asking you to destroy the original?
Cindy:	I have no idea why he wanted to do that.
Sharon:	It doesn't make any logical sense, does it?
Cindy:	Actually it does. Because…
Sharon:	He's not a beneficiary, is he?
Cindy:	He did not want it to go into a trust.
Sharon:	Well, see now there you don't want to make my assumption. My assumption was let's assume there would still be a trust. Even if all we have is a copy. Remember? Let's assume that. Still a trust, and it's up to the judge to decide whether I'm right or wrong. Let's assume that for a minute, okay? Can you do that?
Cindy:	I don't know this. I'm not an attorney.
Sharon:	I'm asking you to assume that even if we had no original will, all we had was the copy that you gave to Mark. That there still would be a trust. Okay, can you assume that?
Cindy:	Okay.
Sharon:	What benefit would there have been to Mark in asking you to destroy the original?
Cindy:	I don't know. I can't speak for Mark.

Sharon: Now…Mark was appointed as personal representative because Paul nominated him as personal
representative, right?

Cindy: Paul and I did together.

Sharon: And that wasn't revoked?

Cindy: No, it wasn't. It was my idea.

Sharon: At the time of the funeral, it was clear at that point
that the divorce had been final before Paul had died,
right?

Cindy: I'm not certain on the exact timeline of when we
found out. I had to call my attorney, who was on
vacation in California. He had to call the judge to
find out what day he had actually signed the papers.
So, I'm not quite certain what day we found out…

Sharon: You wouldn't…have an argument with Mark's
testimony that when he came for the funeral, there
was no question at that point that the divorce had
become final before Paul died?

Cindy: Again, I'm not certain what time. It took a while
to find out if the divorce had been signed.

Sharon: Let me give you what has been marked as Exhibit
14. Now one of the early issues that arose had to
do with an Ameriprise IRA. Is that right?

Cindy: Yes, that's correct.

Sharon: And the dispute arose as to how it was supposed
to be divided?

Cindy: That's correct.

Sharon: And that was because the value of the IRA had
gone down since the time of Paul's death.

Cindy: No, that's not correct.

Sharon: Okay, did the value go up?

Cindy: The dispute was about whether the $93,000 was a fixed number or whether it was a floating number, and if it needs to be done within ten days of that value or if it was done as a floating [number] whenever the transaction took place. Those were the disputes.

Sharon: Okay, this dispute arose because the value of the account decreased.

Cindy: No.

Sharon: All right…tell me then, what was the dispute about how the Ameriprise IRA was to be divided?

Cindy: I hired Diane Prescott to update my trust, and about May or April…

Sharon: I think we're going way too far back. Okay.

Cindy: There is relevance to this.

Sharon: No, I'm sorry, I don't think there is. What we're talking about is shortly after Paul's death…a dispute arose as to how a particular asset was to be divided between you and Paul's estate. Is that correct?

Cindy: That's correct.

Sharon: You didn't like my characterization of the dispute, so I'm asking you to please characterize the dispute in your own words, and the past history isn't relevant.

Cindy: The divorce decree was changed within the last week to be sure that it was…a firm number within ten days. It was one of the last changes made to the divorce decree based on Diane Prescott looking at the divorce decree and [saying], "No way do you want to have this to be an open-ended IRA transfer…you need to put in ten days," and that was changed right before the divorce decree was submitted to the courts.

Sharon: Okay, if you could take a look at Exhibit 14…Can you look at that…tell me if you can identify that, please?

Cindy: This is the information that I offered to Mark when I asked Steve Smith about that transaction.

Sharon: Okay, I'm sorry; this is an e-mail relating specifically to this Ameriprise IRA, right?

Cindy: That's correct.

Sharon: And this is an e-mail you sent to Mark on October 14, 2008, right?

Cindy: I volunteered this information to him.

Sharon: And what you were doing was forwarding from Steve Smith an e-mail…he sent to you [on] to Mark.

Cindy: That's correct.

Sharon: Steve Smith was your lawyer in the divorce.

Cindy: That's correct.

Sharon: And Steve Smith says, "Cindy, I have gone back and reviewed my file notes and the details of the rule 69 marital settlement agreement we reached thru Judith Wolf. The intention was that all of the IRA assets would be divided equally. IRAs are 100% community property; as such, market fluctuations could have affected and undoubtedly did affect these various accounts. Such market variations should not fall solely to one party or another. In other words, the date of determining the equalization amount should be the date of that actual exchange between the accounts not some randomly selected date in the past. Do you see that?

Cindy: Yes, I do.

Sharon: So, your lawyer was saying in essence, "Cindy, I disagree with your interpretation on the Ameriprise IRA account. Right?

Cindy: That's what he's saying.

Sharon: All right. And you sent that on to Mark.

Cindy: Yes, I did.

Sharon: Right…and then he checked with Chuck Hallam, who was Paul's divorce attorney, right? And if you look at the next page…we have from Mark to Cindy, "Cindy, I'm passing on Hallam's response. You know exactly what he has to say without my interpretation or spin." And then he says some other stuff, not terribly relevant and then…we have Chuck Hallam's e-mail. And Chuck's opinion was, "The numbers in the decree were not current. And the $93,338.34 was based on the figures in the decree. It was contemplated that the actual division would be based on numbers on the date of division; therefore, you would need current figures at least through 9/30 to correctly divide the accounts. And then he says the

Caremark pension you need a QDRO for. Okay, so Chuck Hallam is also saying, "Cindy, I disagree with your interpretation of how the Ameriprise IRA is to be divided. Right?

Cindy: That's what he's saying.

Sharon: Okay, so Mark then took the position, "Cindy, I disagree with your interpretation of how the Ameriprise IRA account is to be divided. Right?

Cindy: That's correct.

Sharon: And after he communicated that to you, you cut off communications with him for at least two months?

Cindy: "I don't remember exactly…yes, it's probably similar to that because at that point…

Sharon: That's okay…and he e-mailed you asking you to divide up the IRA and just hold back the disputed portion, right?

Cindy: That's correct.

Sharon: So as to deal with this concern that you had about market fluctuation, right?

Cindy: That's correct.

Sharon: You said, "No, I will not do that. Right?

Cindy: That's correct.

Sharon: Now he also e-mails you and says, "Hey, you know when you going to show a little common courtesy and respond to me so that we can get this moving along?" Right?

Cindy: That's correct.

Sharon: And finally, in January…this is an e-mail that you sent to Mark saying, "I would like to get the IRA resolved today if you have time to do it." Right?

Cindy: That's correct.

Sharon: And you cc your kids on it, right? Even though you don't want your kids to know anything about the estate, right? They're [copied] on there. Yes?

Cindy: That's correct.

Sharon: Yeah. You got mad at him for keeping them advised about the estate issues, right? But it was okay if *you* did it. Correct?

Cindy: I felt I wanted the children to know that I was going to try to get this. I was giving up. I'm giving up the money.

Sharon: So, okay if *you* notify them, but not him.

Cindy: If it's positive.

Sharon: So if it makes you look good then they can know, but if it makes you look not so good they shouldn't know, right?

Cindy: I don't know about that.

Sharon: In August you became aware that…Mark was being appointed as personal representative. Is that correct?

Cindy: That's correct.

Sharon: And at that time you were represented by Diane Prescott, right?

Cindy: That's true.

Sharon: And you did not make any kind of objection to Mark being appointed as personal representative. Did you?

Cindy: No, I did not.

Sharon: Even though you were horrified that he had supposedly asked you to destroy a will. Right?

Cindy: That's correct.

Sharon: Did you ever tell your kids that Mark was stealing from the trust?

Cindy: Throughout this whole time, I have had that suggested to me. And it has been my position that I can't even imagine that Mark would do that to Joe and Kevin and Michelle.

Sharon: Okay, so if Kevin testifies that you've said that all the time that Mark stole from the trust...he is wrong?

Cindy: I'm not going to testify against my son.

Sharon: Well, okay, I guess I misunderstood your answer. Did you ever tell the kids that Mark was stealing money from the trust?

Cindy: No.

Sharon: You would agree that your kids were alienated from you because of your own conduct. Is that right?

Cindy: Partially my own conduct.

Sharon: You fought with Kevin a lot.

Cindy: I think a lot is relative.

Sharon: Okay. He moved out of the house the second he could.

Cindy: No, he lived [there] past the time he was 18.

A Woman of Interest

Sharon: How long?

Cindy: I don't recall the time he left.

Sharon: He preferred to go live with his father, right, when his Dad was alive?

Cindy: Yes.

Sharon: You tried to stop him from having any kind of relationship with the Zimmermanns after his father died, right?

Cindy: No, that's not true.

Sharon: You tried to stop your daughter from having any kind of a relationship with the Zimmermanns after her father died, is that right?

Cindy: No, that's not true. I bought airline tickets to send them to Connecticut.

Sharon: Those are the ones that you are…trying to charge to the estate, right?

Cindy: That's correct.

Sharon: Those were a gift from you, weren't they?

Cindy: No, they were not. The Zimmermanns had asked me to [let them] spend time with…

Sharon: I'm sorry, there was no question. Now you had instructed your first lawyer, Diane Prescott, to write a letter to Mark telling him to not have any contact with the kids, right?

Cindy: That's correct.

Sharon: Let me show you…what's that?

Cindy: That's Michelle writing to Mark about…being unhappy in my home, in our home.

Sharon: And you got *very* upset with Michelle when you saw that she had sent an e-mail to Mark. Is that right?

Cindy: I don't recall about that.

Sharon: When you had your deposition taken, we looked at this e-mail…we say…this is the e-mail from Michelle that she sent him. Your answer: "Yes." And you found out about that e-mail and you were not very happy, right? And you said, "I wouldn't say that." You were happy about the e-mail? You said, "No, I was not happy."

Cindy: That's correct.

Sharon: You weren't happy about her reaching out to her Uncle Mark. Is that right?

Cindy: Well, as I went on to say, you asked me if I screamed and yelled at her about it. I said I don't know, I don't recall if I did that or not.

Sharon: And then I asked you, "Now your daughter was reaching out to Mark [and] you didn't like that, and your answer was, "That's correct."

Cindy: That's correct.

Sharon: So your daughter wasn't supposed to have a relationship with Uncle Mark, was she?

Cindy: I encourage my children to have relationships with people that when they reach out to them that maybe the response would have been, "You know what? Your mom might be under a lot of pressure right now. What can I do to help her?" Maybe I would get a phone call from Mark and [he'd] say, "What can I do to help?"

Sharon: Of course you weren't talking to him, so how could he do that?

Cindy: Well, because I would get e-mails back from him saying, "How dare you call me at 2:00 in the morning."

Sharon: Now that was an e-mail that he sent to you after you had the police call him at 2:00 in the morning after you refused to talk to him for three months, right?

Cindy: The police...

Sharon: Right?

Cindy: The police needed to find out about [Kevin's] truck. I'm with the police. I don't have a choice.

Sharon: Okay. Now you at some point blamed Kevin for his father's death, right?

Cindy: In a heated disagreement.

Sharon: You blamed him for your divorce.

Cindy: In a heated disagreement.

Sharon: And they all went and stayed with Mark for three days when he came to town, so that they could get away from you.

Cindy: Yes, that's true.

Sharon: And you were outside in your underwear, drunk, screaming, and yelling at them.

Cindy: No, I was not outside and I was not drunk.

Sharon: I think you admitted in your deposition that you had been drinking.

Cindy: Yes I did say that.

Sharon: Now you're claiming that Mark should be removed as PR because your son Kevin got in trouble with a truck in December of 2008. Is that right?

Cindy: That's one of the reasons.

Sharon: Okay. This is a vehicle that Kevin's father gave to him to drive before he died.

Cindy: That's correct.

Sharon: Kevin had the keys.

Cindy: That's correct.

Sharon: You demanded them back.

Cindy: That's correct.

Sharon: He refused to give them to you.

Cindy: That's correct.

Sharon: Mark insured it as an estate as an asset of the estate, right? He insured it.

Cindy: As I understand, he did. I don't know, I didn't see the checks.

Sharon: Okay, and you agreed with Kevin that he could keep the vehicle until you could get him something else, right?

Cindy: I don't recall exactly...I went round and round trying to figure out a way to get the truck from Kevin.

Sharon: Okay, but if Kevin testifies that that's the agreement that the two of you had reached about the truck, would you have any reason to disagree with him? Since you don't remember?

Cindy: There were many agreements on how we tried to negotiate of getting the truck from Kevin.

Sharon: So, he took the vehicle out and he did some damage.

Cindy: That's correct.

Sharon: And that's Mark's fault and he was in Connecticut—what, 3,000 miles away?

Cindy: Yes, it is.

Sharon: Okay. Now you're claiming that Mark should be removed as the PR because he did not pay the entire $12,000 family allowance. Is that right?

Cindy: He didn't follow the statutory laws as I understand them.

Sharon: You understand that he made that decision because you were putting the money into a savings account rather than using it to support the kids. Right?

Cindy: That's what I spoke of earlier, when he made that assumption.

Sharon: Let me give you what's marked Exhibit 12 and look at the very last e-mail…the reason he came to that assumption is was because you said, "I'm opening up savings accounts," right?

Cindy: I wanted to get the most return I could on the kid's money.

Sharon: So Mark's assumption that you were putting the money into a savings account rather than using it to support the kids was accurate. Wasn't it?

Cindy: I don't know. I can't speak for Mark.

Sharon: You were putting the money into a savings account, right?

Cindy: Actually, what I did was I had a very special envelope and it was cash. *(crying)* And any time any of the kids spent any of that money I wanted them to know it was their Dad's money. I specifically always handed it to them and said, "This is money from your Dad." I gave my daughter $500 to go to Disneyland and I wanted her to know this was money from Dad and he would want you to go to Disneyland over spring break with Uncle Robbie. So that is absolutely untrue.

Sharon: Okay, so the e-mail you wrote to your kids saying, "I'm opening up a savings account for this money" is inaccurate.

Cindy: No it is not inaccurate.

Sharon: Okay, Mark, when he saw that e-mail, said, "Guys, this is supposed to be for the support of the kids. If it's not for the support of the kids, then I don't think I can pay it under the statute." Is that right? He said, "Give me a little bit more information about why, where this money is going, please." Right?

Cindy: I don't recall an e-mail asking me for anything like that.

Sharon: Okay. Did you ever provide any additional information about why he should continue to pay a family allowance when you are setting up a savings account for the family allowance?

Cindy: We have submitted reams of receipts…

Sharon: Have you, have you…

A Woman of Interest

Cindy: ...of things that I have paid for.

Sharon: Did you submit any information to him?

Cindy: Mark has seen reams of receipts of things that I have...

Sharon: Have you submitted...

Cindy: ...for these children.

Sharon: Did you respond to his request for additional information about what you were doing with the family allowance money?

Cindy: Yes, I think so. In all of the information we have sent to him, it should be pretty clear, very.

Sharon: All right. You were receiving $3,600 a month from Social Security at that point, right?

Cindy: That's correct.

Sharon: And Mark expressed concern that rather than having this money come to you as a family allowance, he would prefer that it ultimately go directly into the trust for the children, right? Wasn't that his concern?

Cindy: I don't remember he and I talking about that.

Sharon: Let me give you what's been marked Exhibit 11. Do you have that in front of you?

Cindy: Yes.

Sharon: You are claiming that Mark should be removed as PR because he has not distributed a Schwab account that was joint between you and Paul.

Cindy: That's correct.

Sharon: And this exhibit is correspondence between Mark and your lawyer providing the evidence that $11,000 improperly went missing out of that account, right?

Cindy: That's correct.

Sharon: And your lawyer asked for that evidence, right?

Cindy: That's correct.

Sharon: And it's because Mark has evidence that $11,000 went missing out of that account that he decided that he can't equally divide that account, right?

Cindy: That's correct.

Sharon: He said, "Look, we can set aside the $11,000 and we'll split the rest of it," right?

Cindy: Possibly, yeah, okay.

Sharon: And you rejected that offer?

Cindy: That's correct.

Sharon: Because you wanted that $11,000, right?

Cindy: Because this is about the fifteenth time I've been asked to front more money to this estate.

Sharon: Right. You took the money out of the account after the divorce decree was filed and the stay was placed on that account, right?

Cindy: That was an arrangement between Paul and I, in a...

Sharon: I am not asking for information from your husband. You, the two of you, weren't even talking at that time, were you?

Cindy: Yes, we were.

Sharon: You were getting along well.

Cindy: I was very concerned for his well being and he knew it. I had reached out to him and asked him, "Please, can I take Michelle? *(crying)* Can we tell her that maybe you got a consulting job and please not continue…"

Sharon: I'm not sure what that has to do with the $11,000, but…

George: Answer the question.

Cindy: We had bills that needed to be paid and Paul was…

Sharon: No, I'm sorry, I don't want testimony about what your husband told you.

Cindy: Oh, okay, I thought you asked me a question.

Sharon: No. Now you understood that in the decree of the dissolution that debts that you incurred after the date of filing were your debts. Is that right?

Cindy: I guess so. I don't really…

Sharon: You understood that, right?

Cindy: I don't really understand what you're asking me.

Sharon: Okay.

Cindy: It's not something that I've been talked to my attorney about.

Sharon: Okay. You took money out of an account that was frozen by the court because you had filed for divorce against your husband, right?

Cindy: It had happened before. That Paul would give me permission…

Sharon: No, I'm sorry, ma'am, please…

Cindy: …to write a check out of the Schwab account.

Sharon:	No, please, you took money out of an account after the divorce decree was filed and the account was frozen, right?
Cindy:	Paul told me…
Sharon:	No, ma'am, yes or no.
Judge:	You can answer the question yes or no.
Cindy:	Yes.
Judge:	Except it couldn't have been a frozen account if you could take money out of it.
Sharon:	Well, okay, fair enough.
Sharon:	It was an account that was ordered by the court to be left alone until the divorce was final, is that correct?
Cindy:	That's correct, but also earlier in another situation…
Sharon:	That's okay, that is okay, ma'am, thanks. You believe that Mark should be removed as PR because he has not agreed with you about the way the Caremark pension is supposed to be divided. Is that right?
Cindy:	I don't really personalize it with Mark…it's not about Mark. It's about this confusion. And I want me and my three children to be able to move…
Sharon:	Okay, you're petitioning to remove him as PR, right?
Cindy:	That's correct.
Sharon:	And you're claiming that he's not acting in the best interest of the estate, right?
Cindy:	In the best interest of my children and [me] and our family.

A Woman of Interest

Sharon: Okay, well the standard is the best interest of the estate. You're not part of the estate, are you?

Cindy: I don't know the terms for that.

Sharon: No, you're not.

Cindy: Okay.

Sharon: So it is…

George: Objection, your honor. Misstates legal relationships.

Judge: Sustained.

Sharon: Okay. Let me go back to the original question. You're claiming that Mark should be removed as PR because he hasn't divided the Caremark pension the way that you want it to be.

Cindy: No, I'm asking to have him removed because he doesn't follow the laws. He breaks laws.

Sharon: You understand that the two of you hired a lawyer that's supposed to work to divide that pension, right?

Cindy: That's correct.

Sharon: And that lawyer was Robert Harrian, right?

Cindy: Yes, he was chosen by Mark.

Sharon: And you agreed with his hiring, right?

Cindy: I was told to send a check for…fifteen hundred dollars. So I followed my attorney's advice and did that.

Sharon: So you agreed to the hiring of Mr. Harrian, right?

Cindy: Yes, I did.

Sharon: Now when Mr. Harrian looked at the matter, he said, "Mmmm, I think there's a problem here because some portion of this Caremark pension was earned by Paul before he was married. Right?

Cindy: Well, actually I heard about that from my attorney. Mark was in speaking to this attorney. The attorney was not giving me equal information. In fact, the last time in court I'm asking for those attorney fees back because he was giving information to Mark and not giving me the same information at the same time. So once again Mark is seeming to have some kind of an inappropriate relationship with someone that's supposed to be taking care of the divorce decree. That's a signed document.

Sharon: Okay, let me show you what's been marked as Exhibit 34 and see if you can identify that for me, please. Have you seen that before?

George: We're having trouble keeping track of the exhibits…can I see what that one is?

Judge: It's the Zimmermann QDRO.

Sharon: Okay, do you have that e-mail in front of you?

Cindy: Yes.

Sharon: In that e-mail that's Mr. Harrian telling your lawyer, "Hey, there's an issue about how the Caremark pension is supposed to be divided," right?

Cindy: Based on George requesting it from a phone call that he got.

Sharon: Right, okay, so he told Mr. Paul you know there's an issue here. I'm not sure how to divide this pension. Right?

A Woman of Interest

Cindy: Yes.

Sharon: And based on that concern about how to divide the pension, Mark said, "You know what, I don't think I can divide the pension the way that on a 50/50 basis," right?

Cindy: That's correct.

Sharon: Because this other lawyer raised an issue and if I do it 50/50 I might have a breach of fiduciary duty with respect to the beneficiaries, right?

Cindy: I can't speak for Mark.

Sharon: Okay, he doesn't get anything out of that pension if it's somehow not divided up the way you want. I mean, he doesn't stand to gain anything, does he?

Cindy: It seems that he gets personal satisfaction out of…

Sharon: Okay, but that's not…

George: Well, your honor…

Sharon: That sounds a little speculative.

George: I object to just an interruption of the answer.

Judge: The answer will stand. I mean if you ask a question and the witness answers it, she is entitled to finish her answer.

Sharon: Sure. I apologize if I cut you off.

George: Well, it's been a common occurrence.

Sharon: Well, I apologize for that, too.

George: Thank you.

Sharon: Is there anything else that you want me to apologize for?

Judge:	Before we continue, though, have you completed your answer? I think your answer were words to the affect of "I think he gets personal satisfaction."
Cindy:	It just seems to me that is just one thing after another. No matter what answer I give, no matter what issue we're talking about, it turns into a conflict, more lawyers, more legal fees. It's just... it never stops. It has never stopped.
Sharon:	Now you're raising an issue about health insurance, right?
Cindy:	That's correct.
Sharon:	That issue was never raised until March of 2009. Is that right?
Cindy:	That's not correct.
Sharon:	There are no documents reflecting that, are there?
Cindy:	No, there are e-mails from about seven days after the funeral when Mark started...
Sharon:	Any that you have submitted as evidence here?
Cindy:	I can't even keep track of all the...the amount of evidence that's been submitted is about six inches deep.
Sharon:	Well, you've actually only got ten exhibits that are here that you've submitted.
Cindy:	There were too many e-mails about health insurance, because Mark was going to cut the health insurance off. I pleaded with him to give me some time to evaluate the options. I had to talk with Susan Goldwater here in town of Hospice of the Valley to find out what should I do in this situation;

A Woman of Interest

we had Blue Cross Blue Shield. I was trying to weigh my options. I was under extraordinary stress and health insurance, as I said in an e-mail to Mark, was very important to Paul and I. As we were in the health industry, I wanted to make sure that I protected my family. I did not want to make a decision when I was extraordinarily under pressure.

Sharon: Isn't it accurate that when you and Mark talked about health insurance, you said, "I will take care of it."

Cindy: No, he insisted that I get on it. And he said, "There was some kind of a quote...well, when do you think you can get around to making this decision?" I'm evaluating the options. Meanwhile I'm going to be getting a refund back from the premium from Blue Cross Blue Shield. The estate's not paying for it.

Sharon: You understood that once Paul passed away, that policy from his employer would terminate, right?

Cindy: I didn't understand any of it. I needed time to process through all this. I had my identity stolen, I had three children that have lost their father, I'm trying to get them in schools. I have more than enough to do on my plate. I didn't think health insurance for my family was something I would have to worry about. *(tearful)*

Sharon: Now you didn't submit any bills for unreimbursed medical expenses until June 17, 2009. Is that right?

Cindy: I have submitted bills from August...I mean, the $2,100 I would assume a reasonable personal representative might think that health insurance cost more than $2,100 for eighteen months for a mother and three children. And I understand my health insurance isn't included, it's for my kids.

Sharon: So my question was: Isn't it accurate that you did not submit any bills for unreimbursed medical expenses to Mr. Zimmermann until June 17 of 2009?

Cindy: I don't remember the first time that I made copies of all the counseling and medical bills that I paid for, for my children.

Sharon: Okay, and that was under a letter from your lawyer, Mr. Paul, right? That you sent those bills?

Cindy: It could have been Diane, it could have been George. I paid for lots of counseling, medical expenses for my children.

Sharon: Okay, now you remember that under the divorce decree you were supposed to submit unreimbursed medical expenses at the beginning of every month and that then you and your ex-husband were to divide those, 56% him, 44% you. Is that right?

Cindy: Yes.

Sharon: And you didn't follow that procedure with Mr. Zimmermann, right?

Cindy: Well, I didn't assume that he was my ex-husband. I thought that agreement was with Paul. I didn't know what to do. Most people have not known what to do when a divorce decree happens the same day that somebody is murdered.

Sharon: Okay, so you waited…

Cindy: Even attorneys have had trouble guiding me on what to do (*crying*). So what I've tried to put is put one foot in front of the other [and] be the best mother

A Woman of Interest

that I could with certainly some mistakes along the way. I have three teenagers and I tried my very best.

Sharon: Are you ready for the next question?

Cindy: Yes. I am.

Sharon: Okay. You submitted medical expenses about nine months after Paul's death to Mark, right?

Cindy: I don't remember. I don't remember every single receipt. I have submitted so many receipts and asked for reimbursement so many times, I'm not going to perjure myself on exactly what receipts I submitted. I have asked for reimbursement many times for storage units, funeral expenses, I mean it just goes on and on.

Sharon: Okay, well let's take a look at Exhibit 10 that your lawyer submitted. Now this June 17, 2007, letter, which is the very first letter on here, reflects, "I'm sending you unreimbursed medical expenses," right?

Cindy: Yes.

Sharon: That's the date of the letter, June 17, 2009?

Cindy: Yes, that's correct.

Sharon: And do you have an understanding that there have been many attempts to try and achieve some sort of global resolution here, those unreimbursed medical expenses a part of that?

Cindy: Oh, absolutely.

Sharon: You have submitted what you call funeral expenses, [which] are plane tickets for your kids to go see their grandparents in Florida, right?

Cindy: They carried their father's ashes to Florida.

Sharon: Okay. Did you tell the kids that that was a gift from you?

Cindy: No, I did not.

Sharon: And those are now being submitted as expenses against the estate.

Cindy: The gift to the children was that I flew out Kevin's girlfriend and her mother to come out to the funeral. I paid about $2,500 or some amount of money...$2,000...expensive airline tickets for them to come out to the funeral. No, I did not say I would take $2,800 to fly my children and their father's ashes to Florida. They asked me if then they could spend some time with the kids and I wanted my children to be able to do that with Paul's family.

Sharon: And now you're submitting that as an expense to the estate.

Cindy: That's correct.

Sharon: You indicated that there has been a lot of delay in this matter, right?

Cindy: That's correct.

Sharon: Would you agree that when you refused to speak to Mark for an extended period of time, that that might of delayed things a bit?

Cindy: Yes...this is after four months of trying to work with him and I was advised to just stop, because of the legal fees of these types of disagreements, where he would ask me a question, I would try to explain it, and then it gets into then let's argue about it.

Sharon: So your refusal to communicate with him might have delayed things a bit, right?

Cindy: I can't speak…I think this will go on forever. No, it will go on until Michelle turns 18, if Mark remains the personal representative.

Sharon: Okay.

Cindy: It will be one thing after another.

Sharon: All right, let me make sure I got an answer to my question. Do you think that not refusing to talk to him for an extended period of time might have delayed things a bit?

Cindy: No, I don't.

Sharon: All right, that's all I have.

Judge: Any redirect?

George: Yes, your honor. Well, no matter when you started talking about health insurance, it hasn't been reimbursed to this day yet, has it?

Cindy: No. It doesn't make any difference when I talk about anything.

George: Well, okay, now no matter when you started talking about the statutory allowances, that was about a year ago?

Cindy: Yeah.

George: They haven't been paid to this day yet, have they?

Cindy: No, they have not.

George: Now how about these unreimbursed medical expenses—maybe it was only several months ago that you documented them all, but have they been paid to this day?

Cindy: No, they haven't.

George: How about the extracurricular activities that you want to give to your children, particularly Michelle. Have they been paid to this day?

Cindy: No, they haven't.

George: How about these funeral expenses that are being contested. Have they been paid to this day?

Cindy: No, they haven't.

George: How about this storage unit? Has it been paid to this day?

Cindy: No, it hasn't.

George: Has anything been paid to this day?

Cindy: I have had one check for $2,100.

George: Well, you were asked some hypothetical questions about what would be Mark's motive to destroy an original will. Do you remember that?

Cindy: Mm-hmm.

George: I'd like for you to assume that there is a statute named ARS 14-3415. Can you assume that with me?

Cindy: Well, I'm not an attorney.

George: Okay, well you were asked this on your cross, and that statute says that if an original will that was last seen in the possession of the testator cannot be found after the testator's death, the testator is presumed to have destroyed the will with the intention of revocation. All right? So can you assume that if the original will couldn't have been found there was a presumption under the law that it was revoked and that the person would have been... that Paul would have been intestate?

A Woman of Interest

Cindy:	I'm assuming that's what you're saying. I don't really understand this.
George:	Okay. Mark didn't explain his reasoning for wanting you to destroy the original will. He didn't explain his legal theory.
Cindy:	No, he just...
George:	Had he been consulting with Ms. Moyer about this theory any theories that he might have?
Cindy:	I don't know.
George:	Okay...he didn't explain this legally?
Cindy:	No.
George:	But he did say that this would eliminate the trust because there would be intestate. Correct?
Cindy:	That's true. He didn't want there to be a trust.
George:	All right, all right. Now you were accused on cross-examination of, I think the word was "supposedly" being told by him that he wanted the original will destroyed. Remember that, supposedly?
Cindy:	That's correct."
George:	Okay, now is there any doubt in your mind that that is what he was asking you to do?
Cindy:	There is no doubt in my mind.
George:	Is that what you told Diane Prescott that very day?
Cindy:	That's correct.
George:	That they are now saying that you are making up later?
Cindy:	That's correct.

George: All right, now you said there was some confusion about when Mark knew that you had the original, whether it was the day of the conversation he asked you to destroy it or earlier. Do you remember that confusion? You weren't allowed to answer what the confusion was?

Cindy: Yes.

George: What is your best piecing together of what happened at this point?

Cindy: Well, I was not certain and Diane wasn't certain if I was going to be filing the probate and whoever filed probate...needed to have the original will. So there was some conversation between Diane and I about whether she should have the original will or if I should.

Sharon: Objection. Hearsay.

Judge: Overruled. You may continue.

Cindy: So that's why I'm not certain if it was in my safe or if Diane and I were having conversations...it was so confusing about whether Joe was going to be the personal representative or what was going on. So that's why I don't want to perjure myself about that.

George: Well, what's your best recollection today about when you told Mark for sure that you had an original will?

Cindy: In the conversation on Wednesday, August 6th.

George: The same conversation [in which] he asked you to destroy it?

Cindy: Yes.

George: That's when he knew for sure?

Cindy: Yes, that I had it.

George: No further questions on redirect, your honor.

Judge: Thank you very much. You may step down. Okay, a couple things strike me before we proceed any further. It's nearly 4:30. I think that I've gotten a real good feeling as to what the parties relative positions are by reviewing the exhibits and having previously reviewed all of the pleadings. And there are a couple of ways we can proceed. And of course it's really up to the parties and I think it's only fair to let you know what the court's perspective on things is it at this point. I do have available a continued hearing date of October 16 at 1:30 p.m. Okay?

So that is certainly available to reschedule the matter and to bring out the additional testimony, which all the parties are absolutely entitled to bring out. I'll tell you I've handled thousands of these cases. The court has basically the fundamental purposes of the probate code to keep in mind whenever it's dealing with a case of this nature. And that's set forth in 14-1102, which indicates that the underlying purposes and policies of the title are to impart simplify and clarify the laws that relate to decedents. To try to discover and make affect of the intent of the decedents. To promote a speedy and efficient system for liquidating the estate of the decedent and making distributions to his successors and to facilitate the use and enforcement of certain trusts.

I think all of the parties would agree here that we have a valid will, no matter where it came from or what the provisions are in the will. We've got a valid will. We have a will that probably should have been modified based on the dissolution proceedings, but wasn't. At least from my review, but the correct personal representative was the individual who was designated in the will and he has been acting under that appointment up to and including the time that the petition to remove him was filed. The only issue that I'm being asked to consider today is really the issue of whether or not a successor personal representative should be appointed. And there is not before the court a petition for instructions as to the meaning of the divorce decree, which this court could certainly do. Whether the language in the decree controls whether or not the spousal allowances are appropriately made and paid. The only thing is, do we need a new personal representative?

Now I have absolutely no doubt from my review of the file that Mr. Mark Zimmermann is fundamentally propelled by his love and concern regarding his two nephews and niece. He's also clearly, as most family members do in situations like this, suffering under the probably the knowledge and the understanding of everything that happened during a very rancorous divorce. I mean, generally families sort of divide up into sub-families when that happens, and prior relationships are modified forever.

Ms. Zimmermann is not only a creditor, but she's been fundamentally impacted by the death of her ex-husband, the handling of the decree of dissolution, the continuous struggles, and I think that she honestly conveyed, when she said that this could go on forever, you know what I've been doing this

A Woman of Interest

long enough to know, they do…go on forever. And if I allow every single petition to go on forever, this estate would be like many others that I see, there is absolutely no money left for the interested parties.

Even if we reset this and come back with all the additional testimony, from all the additional witnesses, whose testimony I can probably anticipate right now because I've heard it all before, I would probably grant the petition. And I would grant the petition because it always in the best interest of the estate to have a personal representative who can fully, fairly, and efficiently deal with all the interested parties, whether they be an ex-spouse entitled to distributions from a decree or young children experiencing problems with their Mom due to the divorce.

In a case like this, I envision coming back on the 16th if we proceeded and having probably four or five more witnesses, maybe not even finishing that day. Further solidifying the parties' positions. Further enhancing the strife, pressure, and strain, and then I'd be in the position where I'd have to make findings of facts and conclusions of law in every single reason that the personal representative was being replaced. And then we'd have to wait 60 more days. And probably spend more money fighting over the form of judgment, and you would not have at that point even resolved the appropriateness and amount of allowances, the distributions still due under the decree, the distributions of the estate that need to be made.

So I'm just going to exercise my inherent authority and advise you that I'm going to grant the petition today. And I'm going to grant it in recognition of the fact that there are so many issues outstanding that the parties have. And they're valid issues that the parties have to be in a position where a neutral, independent, personal representative is making a call on spousal allowances, support, distributions to the trust, distribution of the IRA, distributions of all of the assets under the decree. And by doing this, I hope to preserve a greater amount of the assets for the children, who I believe are the fundamental reasons that everyone is here. And to avoid further family strife. That is only going to cause the recovery period for the kids to go on interminably.

And so I'm not going to consider any requests for attorney fees and costs at this point. I'm basically going to leave everyone in the courtroom unhappy as they leave. But sometimes the court just has to step in on really basic issues, just do it. And then the financial issues you can…the personal representative can bring a petition for instructions in the family court, a petition for instructions in the probate court or hopefully by being in the position of neutral third party can let the parties know his or her position so that these issues can be resolved.

I cannot allow the trauma of the underlying divorce, the tragedy of the horrific murder of Paul Thomas Zimmermann to cause the entire estate to be utilized in contested court proceedings. If additional contested court proceedings are needed on specific issues, then at least the amount of time, energy, and money will be limited. And I do think that

A Woman of Interest

one thing that I see when I look at the docket is that the time between the time of the appointment which occurred August 19 of 2008 and today, there should have been a resolution regarding the distributions under the decree.

And if the parties disagree, then there should have been an immediate petition into the court to say, "Hey judge, you decide." Because you can't leave provisions of decree to go unenforced and unrecognized for lengthy periods of time, particularly in today's economic market where money seems to be evaporate more quickly than anything else. So that's what I'm doing. And I'm going to direct council to submit a proposed form of order for me.

But the reason I cut everyone off at this point was I will require that the successor personal representative be a certified fiduciary. And I still think though that person will charge the estate and I recognize fully that Mr. Zimmermann has donated his time energy and money to this effort at his fiduciary responsibility, that in the long run if we can get these matters solved more quickly and more fairly and people on both sides feel like their case is being fairly represented, that hopefully we can conclude the matter without further court proceedings. What I can do for you right now, if it would provide any assistance, is I could go print off a listing of all of the certified fiduciaries certified by the administrative office of the courts for the parties' information. These can be lawyers, they can have any number of backgrounds, they can be fiduciary agencies.

There should be experience with family court issues here too, though. I think that would be really helpful. But unless the parties would just like to nominate three separate fiduciaries to the court and have the court decide or pick them out of a hat, or if the parties think they could decide on a fiduciary, or whichever way you'd like to do it is fine with me, but I say let's just do it.

George: Your honor, does it make sense to try pick the personal representative who would be the same entity as the fiduciary trustee, the corporate trustee under the trustamentary trust?

Judge: That would require a stipulation and agreement of the parties, because as I review the trust, the will and the trust, right now there is a designated out-of-state corporate trustee who's in first position, and I would have no objection if the parties agreed to have a certified fiduciary step in as trustee. I'd have no problem with that, but since the only thing I'm dealing with today is the personal representative, I think that would go beyond my authority today to twist the parties' arms any further than I'm already doing it. But I mean that would be fine. It makes eminent sense; it would be cheaper to have an agreed-upon fiduciary. There are a lot of really excellent fiduciaries out there that can perform the duties of personal representative and get this estate wrapped up and fund a trust with it.

George: Okay.

Sharon: I have to put my objection on the record.

Judge: Absolutely, and would you like to come back on the 16th? I mean, that's the alternative.

A Woman of Interest

Sharon: Yeah, I mean I think in fairness to my client, he really should be given the opportunity to be heard. This decision—and I understand and respect the reasons for your decision—but in all fairness, my client hasn't had the opportunity to testify. And I think on that basis, I don't think that the petition can be granted without permitting him an opportunity to be heard.

Judge Well, I think it can be utilizing the inherent power of the probate court to make determinations that are in the best interests of the estates. But I'm just telling you this to let you know how I'm going to rule. And I would not cut your client off from testifying if he elects to do that. But I just wanted to let you know that absent something extraordinary that's not in these materials, because I've just gone through I've previously reviewed all of your pleadings, I've previously reviewed the file, the will, the testamentary trust. I reviewed the memo submitted in reference to these proceedings today. And as we've been going through everything, I've been skimming all of your exhibits and all the other documentation. If your client's testimony is just going to be a reiteration of everything here, then all it's going to present to me is more conflict, more disagreements between Mr. Zimmermann and his ex-sister-in-law. And not that anyone is right or wrong, it's just the mere existence of the conflict is what I'm looking at.

It would not be my intention to make any kind of findings of bad faith or improper conduct or anything. Other than just saying the conflict as presented to the court today is sufficient to justify the removal of the personal representative. And the only downside really for your client is that there would have to be any number of findings made if we proceed to the full bore, probably two more days of.

Sharon: What I would like to propose is that you give my client and I maybe five days to let you and opposing council know whether we want to preserve our opportunity to come back and present testimony.

Judge: Okay, and keep that October 16th?

George: I can't do it on October 16th.

Judge: I hate to tell you but I have trials and hearings every single day through the end of December.

George: Okay, well I just can't do it on October 16th. I'm out of the country for over a week. It's the only week I can't do it.

Judge: Okay, I'm just totally unwilling to find myself in the position in this case that I find in so many other cases too we're trying to accommodate counsels' respective schedules, not only with their schedules but with mine, and cause. I mean, I have a trial that we can only do a day a month. It's because there are eight attorneys in it and it's just impossible to schedule for all the attorneys. I'm going to recess the proceedings today. I am going to direct the parties to meet and confer regarding how they would like to select a fiduciary. But I will give counsel five days to determine whether or not the personal representative would like to present evidence at a continued hearing. I think that your client is entitled to that. I've listened to part of the case and I think that's only fair. I also think it's fair sometimes to let the parties know what the court's view is. The bottom line view is the conflict in and of itself justifies a neutral successor, personal representative. We have to get it done; we have to get it done this month. That's the bottom line. Okay?

Sharon: Okay.

Judge: Thank you so much. We're off the record and recess.

George: Thank you.

Ken, I wish I could write you that after the grueling day in court on October 6, 2009, that the personal representative would have heeded the advice of the judge and step down, but this was not the case. As you recall, he had until noon on Friday, October 9, 2009, to consider his options. Mark's attorney Sharon Moyer notified the Superior Court of Maricopa on Friday, October 9, 2009, that "This e-mail is to confirm the request of Mark Zimmermann for a continued hearing in the above entitled matter." Matter PB2008-002158/Zimmermann.

Oh my gosh. We could hardly believe it. More preparation, more witnesses, more time, more energy, more money.

It is true that on January 18, 2010, the State of Connecticut Judicial Branch considered the bar complaint I filed. According to their letter dated January 19, 2010, "The panel carefully reviewed the information submitted and made its determination without a hearing. The panel determined that no probable cause exists that the respondent committed misconduct. Further, based on this determination, the grievance panel has dismissed this complaint and will take no further action."

It was quite possible I could lose again in the State of Arizona. My former brother-in-law went into great detail about my supposed lack of credibility in his response to the State of Connecticut. He pleaded that my integrity and credibility or lack thereof should be factored into their consideration of my bar complaint. All in public records for the rest of my life.

We prepared for the hearing. We deposed only one witness, Diane Prescott. On October 30, 2009, at 9:02 a.m., the deposition began. It ended at 9:11 a.m. George L. Paul, LLP, asked the questions. Kristi M. Morley, Esq., represented opposing counsel. Frankly, Kristi Morley seemed distracted. It seemed she was there only to relay the testimony of Diane Prescott.

This is an excerpt of her exact testimony:

George Paul: Could you state your name for the record, please?

Diane: Diane Prescott.

George: Ms. Prescott, I'm George Paul, as you know. I'm going to be asking you some questions this morning. If there's anything I ask you that you don't understand, would you let me know?

Diane: I will.

George: Thank you. Are you a practicing attorney?

Diane: I am.

George: Have you ever had Cindy Zimmermann as a client?

Diane: I have.

George: And just roughly, what's the background of when you started representing Cindy?

Diane: Cindy and I got together at the beginning of the year to do estate planning.

George: For Cindy?

Diane: For Cindy.

George: When you say at the beginning of the year, what year are you talking about? Last year? '08?

Diane: '08. I did her estate planning documents. I also reviewed her proposed settlement agreement and decree for her divorce.

George: Were you representing her when her ex-husband Paul was murdered?

Diane: I was representing. We had an ongoing relationship at that time.

George: All right. So you had just kind of finished the... estate planning and then you weren't really doing anything active, but you had a relationship with her, and then Paul was murdered; is that accurate?

Diane: That's accurate.

George: Did you...start up discussions with Cindy again at that time?

Diane: Yes.

George: What was the topic of those discussions?

Diane: Cindy called me on the issue of his death and... what was happening with the police inquiry. She knew that I am a probate attorney. So she asked me about what a probate would be in terms of his estate. And so we talked about that.

George: Okay. Now, did you ever have occasion to talk to Cindy's former brother-in-law Mark Zimmermann?

Diane: I did.

George. Could you tell us the circumstances of those? Were they phone calls or face-to-face calls?

Diane: In August I received some e-mails from Mark. And the e-mails indicated that he understood that I was helping Cindy with questions about the probate of Paul's estate. And the e-mails were very pointed. And they were, "Do you have the original will?"

George: Okay.

Diane: So those were the questions. And I did get a chance to talk to him on the phone. He e-mailed me at my office...and I spoke to him on the phone.

George: Let's focus in on that phone call. I assume it was just the two of you on the phone?

Diane: It was.

George: And can you in any way help us with the date approximately?

Diane: It was approximately August 4 of 2008.

George: And what happened in the phone conversation?

Diane: He introduced himself. And I expressed my condolences for the death of his brother. He asked if I had Paul's original will.

George: Okay.

Diane: And I told him that I didn't have the original will.

George: Anything else in that conversation?

Diane: He was focused on the original will.

George: All right. Did you ever have any other discussions with anybody about the will?

Diane: I did.

George: And what was that?

A Woman of Interest

Diane: On August 6 Cindy called me…and she reported to me that she had had a conversation with Mark, and Mark had asked her to destroy the original will.

George: Okay.

Diane: And the words were, "Get rid of the original will." And my reaction to that…and she wanted my advice. My reaction—I was shocked. I said, "Cindy, I'm shocked. He's an attorney. And that's nothing that he should ever ask you to do." I said, "The original will is a document. Needs to go before the court in probate. And if there are any questions about the will, they should be determined by the court, but you cannot destroy the will. You'd be subject to contempt of court. And I can't represent you if you do that."

George: Anything else happen in that conversation that you can remember?

Diane: I think I recommended to Cindy that this was so serious she should consider a bar complaint.

George: Okay. No further questions.

There were also no further questions from Kristi M. Morley, Esq. We all left the Lewis and Roca building, 40 North Central Avenue, Phoenix, Arizona.

Ten minutes later I got the phone call I had been waiting on, had spent a fortune on: George called to tell me, "Mark Zimmermann is stepping down as personal representative."

Finally, *finally*, he would be out of the picture, and I could get on with my life.

Hugs, your friend, Cindy

THE MOST IMPORTANT
CHAPTER: GRATITUDE

Dear Ken,

At some point I must stop. The book has to come to an end, doesn't it? It is difficult for me to find that place, the end. I am afraid I will have forgotten to mention someone and the kindness and help they have shown me.

While there have been challenges, there have also been so many joys, so many friends who helped me along the way. If I could ask one thing of you, it would be to read the entirety of this chapter, because this is the most important part of my life story thus far.

I've mentioned to you before, Ken, about my love of learning. One of my favorite gifts Paul gave me every year was VIP tickets to the series "Unique Lives and Experiences," one of the top women's lecture series. Founded in 1992, it was one of the first of its kind in the "talk-theater" concept. Its mission was to meet women's demands for intelligent entertainment and meaningful issue-driven discussion.

With VIP tickets I had the opportunity to participate in private receptions for such lecturers as actors Mary Tyler Moore and Lauren Bacall, civil rights activist Coretta Scott King, television news icon Lesley Stahl, and poet Maya Angelou. Paul always bought me two tickets so that I could invite a friend.

A Woman of Interest

Because of my interest in "Unique Lives and Experiences," it was natural that I would be drawn to the Artist-in-Residence Series at the exclusive Lon's at the Hermosa Inn in Paradise Valley, Arizona. You remember, Ken? This was the series that brought us together. Hosted by award-winning author Pam Swartz, the evening is similar to "Unique Lives and Experiences," except even better, which is certainly why I was intrigued by it. The evening includes a pre-dinner wine reception, where guests mingle with the featured artist. Participants then enjoy a sumptuous four-course dinner designed especially for the occasion by Lon's executive chef.

Every Artist-in-Residence evening I have participated in, I've had the opportunity to meet and make new friends. The community seating of eight or ten guests together prompts lively, interesting conversation. I recall one evening, my guest Gabriele Bertaccini and I shared dinner with George Benson and his wife, Johnnie. Later in the evening George sang a short melody at our table. It was just delightful. LUDVIC, the internationally renowned painter and sculptor, was the guest speaker that evening. He and his wife Lauren were fascinating to listen to as they shared stories of their art-filled lives. Friends now, I like to think.

On the night cowboy artist Gary Carter was the guest speaker, Wednesday, October 13, 2010, I met Sheila and Mike Ingram. We had wonderful conversation as we shared stories about Montana and heaven only knows what else. At the end of the evening, I handed Mike my business card, which I always enclose in a fabric envelope from The Cloth Envelope Company. This one happened to be a stars and stripes fabric. He looked at me and said, "You are an angel sent by God." I laughed and said, "I hardly think so!"

He said, "Seriously, Cindy, I need your help. I'm planning an event and could really use your help." It had to do with the Joe Foss Institute. As I recall, I told him I would call him and do whatever I could.

As I had not heard of the Joe Foss Institute before I went home and asked a friend, Lisa James, "I've been asked by a Mike Ingram to help with this event—do you know him or anything about it?"

I learned that Joe Foss was a well-respected national treasure: leading fighter ace of the U.S. Marine Corps during World War II, Medal of Honor recipient, General in the Air National Guard, governor of South Dakota, the first commissioner of the American Football League, and a television broadcaster. In 2001, Foss and his wife Donna "didi" Foss founded the Joe Foss Institute, with a goal to teach patriotism, democracy, public service, integrity, and an appreciation for America's freedoms to children in schools and classrooms throughout the country. Although Foss died in 2003, "didi" and her distinguished board have kept things running smoothly ever since.

Lisa assured me that Mike was a great guy and the Institute was indeed a worthy cause. In fact, she and her husband Gordon James were involved in the event. This was the beginning of my being a part of the team that organized the first annual Stars and Stripes Classic (hence the earlier connection to my stars and stripes envelope)—a dinner and live auction to celebrate and advance the Institute's mission. This year, "didi" Foss' birthday would be celebrated as well.

Political activist and philanthropist Foster Friess hosted the event, which featured a line-up of special guests, including Donna "didi" Foss, Foster Friess, U.S. Senator Jon Kyl, Arizona Governor Jan Brewer, U.S. Representative Trent Franks, U.S. Representative-elect Ben Quayle, Alaska Governor Sarah Palin, Dr. James Dobson of Focus on the Family, Lieutenant General William G. Boykin, Vice President Dan Quayle, Medal of Honor recipient Fred Furguson, CNN Correspondent Alex Quade, and many others. Lee Greenwood, Erin Kalin, Harry Luge Jr., Nancy Schulze, and the U.S. Naval Academy Women's Glee Club provided the special entertainment.

It seems the challenge was there was so much excitement for the event, Mike and the then President of the Joe Foss Institute, Robert Paulk, just needed another pair of hands to help get the final details in place. They seemed to think I could be that extra pair of hands. The event was just around the corner, on November 13, 2010.

I was happy to help. I came to learn that during the course of the evening, many would be honored, including several Medal of Honor recipients and military leaders. Public servants, veterans, firefighters, police officers, and educators were to be recognized for their profound contributions. I became more and more emotionally involved in the event.

I had been looking for my own way to thank the public servants who had helped my family. With the date so close, it was going to be a challenge to find a corporate sponsor. Somehow, I had the idea that my company, Writing In Style, should be the sponsor. Mike Ingram and Robert Paulk tried to talk me out of this very big donation more than once.

My heart was set on it. The thought of having everyone in the room handwrite a note to be sent along with the flowers to veterans around the state was something I just *had* to do.

I swear this is how things transpired: I called Mike and Bob, excitedly telling them I had found a sponsor, but she insisted she needed to talk to them on a conference call before she agreed. We set up the three-way call and I said, "You guys, it's me! That woman is *me*. I really, really want to do this." I then explained how and why I was so grateful for the exact people the event would honor that evening. Finally, they conceded and agreed that Writing In Style could be a sponsor.

More than 600 handwritten notes were written that evening. There were Cloth Envelope Company stars and stripes envelopes throughout the room, with sprigs of rosemary at every place setting. I was thrilled to be able to include my dear friend police advocate

Natalie Summit at my table, to express my gratitude in some small way for all she had done for me.

Now what to give "didi" Foss for a birthday gift? Somehow along the way of planning the event we had talked about fountain pens and calligraphy. I visited my friend Jay Sadow of Scottsdale Pen. He helped me find just the perfect gift, a starter calligraphy fountain pen set. "didi" wrote me in her thank-you note that it was a perfect gift.

I am so very grateful for the many friendships I made in being a part of this wonderful event. During the course of the evening, I met Vernon Parker, then a councilman for Paradise Valley and former mayor. As usual, I worked handwritten notes into our conversation. He took me by surprise when he agreed that he loved handwritten notes, too. In fact, he thought it would be a good topic for a radio show he co-hosted.

I was honored to be invited, but became concerned about whether or not I should talk with him about my recent "headlines." I talked with a friend about it, who concurred that I needed to be open: "Cindy, you really have no choice. He is a public figure, running for office. You need to tell him." While it's a burden I must manage, I don't think it's fair to not let others know the risk that someday the ugliness will resurface and they might unknowingly be associated with me.

You see, that is the thing about character assassination. Character assassination by definition is when an attempt is made to tarnish another's reputation with misleading half-truths or presenting an untrue picture of a targeted person. The damage can last a lifetime, affecting one's personal and professional life. While it's a burden I must manage, I don't think it's fair to ask someone else to bear the brunt of it, especially someone who is offering to help promote my passion, the handwritten note.

So I explained to Vernon Parker about the past few years. He was very gracious and said not to give it a second thought. It seems as a seasoned politician he'd had his own share of public untruths.

We did the radio show. He became a part of the Writing In Style video series. He was kind enough to share his story of his time serving in the White House for President George H.W. Bush. In fact, in a recent letter, the president lent his name and support to his campaign for Congress in Arizona's newly created Congressional District 9. I am grateful for Vernon Parker's generosity, consider him a friend, and hope he thinks the same of me.

I knew when I decided to focus all of my time once again on the handwritten note and Writing In Style, I was going to have many similar conversations explaining the past few years. It seems only fair to offer others a "pass." I had been advised that at some point there would be a reporter who would put the pieces of my story together, and it would be best for me to write my story from my perspective first.

I was trained as a hospice volunteer and learned about grieving, loss, and death. I've learned firsthand. This is an exercise I participated in to guide me to try to be as compassionate and caring for the patients and families I would come to work with as a volunteer and ultimately an employee of Hospice of the Valley. Based on "A Grief and Bereavement Exercise for Small Groups" by Reverend Ronald R. Peak and Reverend James C. Wooldridge, the concept started with 20 slips of paper. On the first five, we wrote the five people most important to us. The next five, we wrote the five activities we liked to do most. On the next five, we wrote the five possessions we liked most. And finally, on the last five, we wrote the places in nature we valued. As the exercise continued, a story was told and participants learned how it is to slowly but surely learn how to lose all of the things most important to them. The participant learned this is how a patient can feel as they experience end of life.

I think of this exercise quite often. I experienced tremendous loss here and there. Certainly I lost friends that I thought would always be friends. There are always two sides to every story. I must admit I lost some faith in those who knew details of Paul's murder but chose to look the other way. There were possessions, material things, I valued but no longer have. Activities and places in nature for some time could no longer bring me joy; in fact I couldn't bear to be around.

This is the note I would like to close my book on. It's not about the people, places, things that I *lost*. It's about the people, places, things that were *helpful* to me. I am eternally grateful that Diane Prescott was there for me and willingly testified under oath about our discussions of the original will of the Paul Thomas Zimmermann estate.

And what now with my life? Most importantly, service to others. After my first divorce, I started a Brownie troop, thinking it would help me move forward. It did. Those precious young ladies looked to me to help them earn their badges. I've always found service to be very rewarding; certainly in times of challenge it has helped me to take my mind off of my own concerns. More recently I've been honored to volunteer with Hospice of the Valley, SAARC, Make-A-Wish, Dining Out for Life, Anixter Center, Fresh Women's Start, COAR, Actors Theatre, Girl Child Network, The Joe Foss Institute, and the Dodie Londen Excellence in Public Service.

I am grateful for the many organizations that have asked or accepted my gifts in one way or another. One of my favorite memories is that of Mercy Musomi of Kenya, East Africa. I met her through a friend, George McDonald. She was visiting Arizona representing the "Girl Child Network." I was asked to have a rather impromptu fundraiser for her. As I recall, it was shortly after Paul had passed away. I was more than happy to host the gathering in my casita.

Mercy and I recognized a kindred spirit in each other with each moment we spent together. As my lifetime collection of photographs of my family and friends had become difficult for me to look through, she reminded me to appreciate them. She shared with us that most of the girls she tried to help had never even seen a picture of themselves, and were unable to recognize their own beauty.

I was proud of my son Kevin that night of the fundraiser, as he went to the store and found a camera and copier for Mercy to take back with her to Africa. Mercy was kind enough to let my book club send many copies of the book "The Education of Little Tree" written by Asa Earl Carter (under the pseudonym Forrest Carter). It was my hope that the experiences and friendships I have had with my book clubs would be passed on to the young ladies in Africa. Mercy has told me that, indeed, her young ladies have been empowered by our exchanges.

I realized that now traveling, exploring the world, and meeting people would be an interest I would need to put on hold for a while. Long known for my love of five-star experiences, who is to know if these are ever to return? First and foremost, my attention to the final years of my children living at home was to be enjoyed. We have had many wonderful experiences together; just goes to show one doesn't need to travel to Dubai, Thailand, Vietnam, Ireland, England, France, Spain, Belize, Africa, The Bahamas, England, Germany, Italy, or Kuwait to have a good time. I savor all of my memories of these travels and the people with whom I traveled.

I am grateful for the many friends who would travel to be with me—Carol Neiger, Sylvia Torres Underhill, Kathyrn Duncan, Lynn Reilly, Barb Dillman, Cathy Muehlberger Jarzemkoski, Becca Istas, Sherry Meyers, Martha Walker, Patty Crutchfield—when it was close to impossible for me to leave town. They came to me to make sure we laughed and loved, making more wonderful girlfriend memories, because truly girlfriends are absolutely one of my favorite things in my life. I am fortunate I have lost very few friends.

I am beyond grateful for the many dear things the Blank and Matney families have done for my family and me. Many, many times Carmen and Michael Blank would be waiting at their front door to listen to the unraveling of my life. They have always given me a safe place to share my tears, laugh when there wasn't much to laugh about, and continue to try to help me move forward.

I am known for always traveling with a load of books. Books are my friends, but in my time of crisis I lost a good number of years of reading. One, there was no extra time to read anything of pleasure; there were too many legal documents to navigate. Two, I couldn't concentrate long enough to read. Until I found the book "Peaks and Valleys" by Spencer Johnson, a brilliant short parable that shows readers how to stay calm and successful even in the most challenging of environments. I bought many copies of that book and sent them to my friends and family, thanking them for their help over the past years.

Giving gifts, a long favorite joy of mine, also needed to be set aside. It seems I've taken far more than I've given in the past years. I'm sure I've missed birthdays, anniversaries, celebrations—all things I so enjoyed celebrating in earlier years. My apologies for missing those special times in those whose lives I treasure. We'll make up for it, don't you worry!

Speaking of books, I don't recall if I have written of our mutual friend, Larry Siegel. I will have to revisit my writings, but I mustn't forget him. Larry is the community relations manager at the North Scottsdale branch of Barnes and Noble, one of my favorite stores in the world. He is known to be generous with his contributions to our community and his wisdom. Somehow or another we became friends. Maybe because I was always in Barnes and Noble bugging him!

Larry gave me the gift of a safe haven. You see, Ken, when it seems the world is gossiping about every detail of your life, it is very unsettling to not know who "really knows" and who doesn't. While I wanted so much to move on, it was difficult with the media coverage and, of course, the gossip. I tried to maintain myself, focus on the tasks at hand (like my business, Writing In Style), and seeing Larry from time to time. Outside of getting a divorce, I didn't mention my personal upsets.

I remember after many months, for some reason I decided to confide in Larry that there were some upsetting things going on in my life. His response, "I know, Cindy, I've known all along. I just wanted you to have a place you could go and not have to think about everything." Just a wonderful gentleman and the dearest of friends. Thank you, Larry, for so very much.

I am forever indebted to my many friends of the Echardt Tolle New Earth group, led by Peter Davis. We spent many Sunday afternoons trying to incorporate the wisdoms of Echardt Tolle's books into our lives, and many a Friday and Saturday sharing laughs and fun. Kim Shipway, Renee Smith, Debbie Black, Denise Aguirre, Jett Yvonne McFadden, Debbie Good—thank you, dear friends.

The holidays were filled with many wonderful traditions. The Christmas season was always very special. Paul and I enjoyed writing our holiday letter to friends and family. We enjoyed the annual professional family photograph. We enjoyed spending Christmas Eve together wrapping the kids' gifts, writing the letter from Santa telling each of the kids why Santa was proud of them that year. Christmas morning was especially fun with mounds of gifts. The stockings, cookies for Santa, and the reading of Santa's letter were all part of our Christmas morning tradition.

Typically, my brother and sister traveled to Kansas City to celebrate the Christmas season. My brother stayed in Phoenix in 2007, my first Christmas alone. It was agreed Paul would have the kids our first year apart as a family. It would be Paul's last Christmas. He traveled with the children to Florida to visit his family.

My brother insisted he would not leave me behind to spend Christmas alone, even though I insisted I would be fine. I had just moved into my casita, I had plenty to do. But he wouldn't take no for an answer.

He showed up at my house with a fake Christmas tree, a case of wine, food, movies, and heaven knows what else and said, "Don't really care how we do this or don't do this, but we're spending

Christmas together. You're not going to be alone." How do I ever begin to thank him for this act of kindness?

My friends and family have been certain I haven't missed celebrations even in times when I didn't really feel like celebrating. It takes a lot for me not to want to celebrate! My 50th birthday in 2008 certainly wouldn't be the celebration of years gone by. But my friends and family made sure there was a barbecue, a party, and I wasn't alone. By this time we were able to listen to music at the party again. Thank you, Cathy Muehlberger Jarzemkoski, Jean Beattie, Jim Dudley, Jody Reyes, Anne Snyder, Debbie and Paul Castaldo, my brother and sister, and my children for making it a special day.

Ironically, Cathy Muehlberger Jarzemkoski would travel back to Kansas City after my 50th birthday celebration only to fly back out to Phoenix for Paul's funeral service. How does one ever thank a friend for something like this? She has her own family and obligations, yet she made two trips to Phoenix in two weeks. I am humbled by her acts of kindness.

For a couple of years I just couldn't listen to music. The words, the lyrics were just too painful, bringing my emotions to the surface, tears and all. There are two incidents that helped bring music back into my life.

First, I had attended my spiritual church with Carmen Blank and Anne Dunlap. Jessika Murphy was singing that Sunday. She sang her heavenly song, "I Will Make a Difference." The words and her beautiful voice were angelic to me. For some reason, that song, her voice, that moment in time was the day my soul could open up to music again. I was moved to tears. I reached out to her, asking for several copies to give to my friends and family for a holiday gift; Christmas was just a few days away. Jessika made it happen, though I recall it was a bit of an imposition for her. She was also kind enough to record this song and our story in the Writing In Style video series, an A to Z handwritten tour of the alphabet on my website.

Second, my hiking friend, Ken Spohn. We spent a lot of time hiking and talking of every subject in the world, I do believe. I remember one night I shared with him that I couldn't listen to Billy Ocean's "Caribbean Queen" song because of the memories of Paul. I remember his words exactly: "Let's get 'er done."

He found the song on his computer. We listened to the song together. It wasn't easy, but he helped me do it. Then he asked, "One more time?"

"One more time," I responded. I can now enjoy the song without the pain, just remembering the good times it brought me. Thank you Ken, Carmen, Anne, and Jessika: music is back in my life.

Moving. Each time I had to move or move things, my friends were there to help me. I don't know if there is a worse request than asking friends to help you move! Thank you, Martha Walker, Nicholas Walker, Mary Kozul, Mladenka Zovko, Barbara Bond, Jean Beattie, and yes, my brother and sister yet again.

Of course, material possessions one treasures must be released as life ends or as the space we live in becomes smaller. Because of my family's love for books, we have many. I remember someone asking me once, "Have you actually read all of these books?" The answer was yes. They jokingly further asked, "Even this one, 'Sober for Life'?" Giggle, giggle.

When downsizing, I gave many books to a charity. As she was looking through them, a friend noticed one in particular and said, "I don't think you'll want to give this one away." It was "Arizona Getaways for the Incurably Romantic," written by Pam Swartz. Of course, the fact that my friend Pam wrote the book is important to me. But more important were the words written inside the cover "Cindy-Happy Valentine's Day 2003! Let's try all of these places! I love you, Paul." This story is featured in the Writing In Style video series. It is absolutely one of my favorite stories, favorite books, and Pam is a favorite friend.

The point is this. If the inscription in the book would have been e-mailed, texted, tweeted, or put out into the universe using whatever the latest technology going is, I would have not known for sure that it came from Paul. Similar to the e-mail sent to me on my 50th birthday, simply stating, "Happy Birthday." I don't know for certain whether Paul sent it or if someone else did. It will always be an uncertainty who had Paul's computer that night.

But this writing, *his* handwriting, I know for certain came from him. I know for certain, in that moment of time, in the year 2003, he was still intending to take incurably romantic getaways with me. No one can distort that memory of us. It is mine to treasure, which brings me to my final love, the hand-written note.

My dear friend Kelly Ehley, I guess her job title is personal assistant, but I call her COO, and she refers to me as CEO. This is a big corporation, this Writing In Style. Can you imagine being *my* personal assistant? That has to make you laugh! I am indebted to her for her generous spirit and always cheering me on. We have a tight non-disclosure agreement, so I can't disclose really exactly what goes on during our working or non-working hours!

I am grateful that Paul Messinger of Messinger Funeral Homes long ago agreed my CZ Custom Gift Design products were worthy of his upscale gift showroom. It was my hope that grieving families would find solace in my products. I created samples of my products and delivered them for display. As I was a volunteer at Hospice of the Valley at the time, it seemed a natural connection. Little did I know that I would later be a person in grief getting comfort from that display.

I liked to include photos with the wording on my gifts. For some reason, at the time I used a photo of my father I particularly liked. On a ceramic book, I attached the following:

"As the chapters
In our stories
continue to unfold,
the gifts you gave us
will forever echo
on the pages of our hearts.
Reluctantly we bid you farewell,
until we meet again."

Why is this so important to me? When the world, my world is shifting, it's been my experience that the universe, God—whatever "title" makes one feel comfortable—the angels on the other side, the angels on this side show up, give us signs to let us know we are not alone. My collection of gifts would be such a sign.

Years had passed, and as I sat in the Messinger Funeral Homes showroom with my children and some of Paul's family (I don't recall who exactly), discussing Paul's ceremony and cremation, another miracle would occur. Never in a million years would I have imagined this moment for my family. As I was now technically not Paul's wife, technically I did not have a say in any of the arrangements, although I was still my children's mother. In some ways they were looking to me for guidance—or maybe they weren't. I don't know. It was all so very confusing. One thing was for certain, I didn't want to make things worse. How could things possibly get worse?

So I was in this showroom of sorts. I was in a void. A non-place. I don't know what to call it. For some reason, I looked around the room and to my utter surprise there on a credenza were my CZ Custom Gift Design products. My father, who had since passed, was looking at me. Gift after gift, he was looking at me through the photos, assuring me, in my mind, that everything was going to be okay.

I want you to understand the magnitude of this miracle. This was a new building. A beautiful new building with many, many showing rooms; more than twenty. What are the odds that we would be led to this particular room, this particular day, to find products I hadn't been selling or seen for many, many years?

Yes, it was a message, a sign, from my father, from Paul, that somehow this would all turn out all right. Not just okay, but extraordinary; that was the way Paul always made it for me and our children.

I hope I have shared enough stories with you to help you understand why the handwritten note is so very important to our world. If not the world, maybe you have come to understand why it is so very important to *me*. Truly, without it I don't know that I would have survived. My mother deserves some of the last words written in my book.

From the moment I was born, she has tried to teach me right from wrong, how to work hard, how to be a nice lady. You can well imagine she had her work cut out for her! She made sure we attended Sunday School and Methodist church services each weekend. She made sure we were involved in community activities. She tried to give us every opportunity she could. There is never a doubt in my mind that my mother loves me, my brother, my sister, and her grandchildren.

My mother grew up in a small town Wellsville, Kansas. She is a simple woman, so being the mother of someone like me couldn't be easy. Though in all fairness, she is the one that taught me to reach for the stars, nothing is impossible! I was in 4th grade, writing a report about Harry S. Truman. It was a difficult year for my family, as my parents were getting a divorce.

I remember my mother liking that Mr. Johnson was my teacher, a good male role model. I remember liking him as my teacher because he was blonde and gorgeous! Plus, he ignited my love for gymnastics, as he was the coach. I still have the little gymnastics uniform I wore for our school team. Incidentally, I still have the handwritten report. Truth be known, I was very impressed with Mr. Truman as well!

Unbeknownst to me, my mother wrote Harry S. Truman, a resident of Independence, Missouri, asking if I might be able to visit him. Unfortunately, Mr. Truman was no longer accepting visitors because he was quite elderly. He did take the time, though, to write me a letter and sent along a book with his writing in it. So you see, this passion of books, writing, and reaching for the stars, is entirely my mother's fault!

In 2007 and 2008, my mother reinforced my appreciation for the handwritten note. Every single day, for one year, my mother wrote me a letter, sent it through the postal service. She believed that if every day I had to get out of bed, leave my apartment, walk to the mailbox, and find written words of love and encouragement, the letters would keep me going. She was right, yet again. Her letters did indeed keep me going.

On a serious note, I cannot imagine how difficult the past years, maybe even my entire life, has been for my mother. I seem to continuously find myself in situations that require attorneys, police officers, psychologists, accountants, medical teams, and more to help me. The combination of events and personalities has been beyond most everyone's comprehension. But my mother has shared that her faith in God is what keeps her believing her oldest daughter will be just fine. Thank you, Mom. I love you dearly.

Because of her influence, I continue to extol the virtues of the handwritten note. It can have such power, such influence.

I believe this to be the most dramatic and powerful story I can share with you about my experiences with the handwritten note. On August 27, 2008, I was so moved by Joe Biden's speech to the nation as he accepted the nomination for vice president of the United States of America. As I have always been interested in politics, both Republican and Democrat, it was only natural that I would be watching Joe Biden on television. It would also be natural because I had met him briefly at the Democratic convention in Chicago in 1996.

As I watched Joe Biden's speech on television the night before, I was very moved by his words. He spoke of his mother and of his father, who always told him, "Champ, when you get knocked down, get up. Get up." I felt compelled for my kids to hear and see me do the same thing. Change. Yes, change was everywhere in 2008. It was the mantra of Barack Obama's presidential campaign. Everybody claimed they wanted change. I had to agree.

How much longer could I survive the legal nightmares, the emotional destruction of my family? I was *so* ready for change. Change I would get. Most of us do, from moment to moment. Our interpretation of that change is up to us.

I woke up the next morning, August 28, 2008, with a determination to take my kids—physically take my kids—to see Barack Obama accept the nomination for president of the United States of America in Denver, Colorado. Somehow I felt certain the energy of such a dramatic event would have a positive effect on all of us.

I reached out to Representative Kyrsten Sinema of the Arizona House of Representatives District 15. We had met each other a few times at various events in Phoenix. I consider her a friend. I hope she does me as well.

My e-mail was simple. At 6:20 a.m. on Thursday, August 28, 2008, I wrote Kyrsten, "Is there any chance at all that you can get 4 tickets to tonight's event in Denver? My three children and I have been through unbelievable circumstances in the past six weeks. I would LOVE to have them experience firsthand that no matter our personal dilemma; there are those in much greater need than we are. We, as Americans, have much to be grateful for, and Barack is one of those blessings. I am in Phoenix, so I would need to get airline tickets in place if you can help us. Thank you so much for your time in even responding to my e-mail. Cindy. P.S.: Hope you are in Denver."

Her response came just 17 minutes later, at 6:37 a.m. "I can try." I think these three words are some of the most powerful in the world. "I can try." They imply an intention of extending one's self for another. Not promising, not over-delivering or under-delivering, just a willingness to try. I am very, very grateful to Kyrsten Sinema.

I know a "yes" when I read one. I began the process of getting airline tickets to Denver to see the next President of the United States accept the nomination. We did, indeed, get to see the nomination.

I don't know if this trip had the intended effect on my children or not. They were long used to me getting these impulses to travel or experience something I thought could be life-altering. Who knows? I know *my* life was altered by the feeling, the energy, of hope and change in Denver, Colorado.

Now fast forward to January 8, 2010. Vice President Joe Biden's mother passed. I felt compassion for the vice president, most importantly because this man, this human being, just lost his mother. I also felt bad for him because he was under a lot of pressure from the media at the time. It seems, to me at least, that sometimes we forget our public servants are human beings.

I wanted to let Vice President Joe Biden know that I had been impacted by his mother and him. Once again, I reached out to Representative Kyrsten Sinema. I asked her if she would forward an e-mail to the vice president expressing my condolences. I included a photograph of us together at the 1996 Democratic Convention and a photograph of my family at the Denver Democratic Convention. Representative Sinema responded that she would—and she did forward the e-mail to the White House.

I didn't hear back from the vice president. I felt certain I would. I wanted to be certain my message reached him. As you know by now, it is important to me that those who have helped me understand my gratitude. One not to give up, I sent the exact same condolences in a handwritten note, with the same photos, in a special fabric envelope from The Cloth Envelope Company, to the White House. This time I got a response. I heard back on March 29, 2010, from the vice president of the United States of America.

I hope that my message doesn't get lost here in a division of politics. I didn't share it with you to make it about politics. Selfishly, I shared it with you in hope that you might understand how important the handwritten note is and the power it has compared to an e-mail. Most importantly, it has the power of courage. I quote Vice President Biden from his eulogy: "She believed in us, so how could we do less?" Mr. Biden went on to say, "Mom taught us that courage is not defined by the lack of fear, but by the willingness to act despite our fear." I thank you one more time Kyrsten Sinema, Vice President Biden, and Catherine Eugenia Finnegan Biden.

I'm sorry to report the stationery industry—naturally near and dear to my heart—as a whole is in trouble, the United States Postal Service is in crisis, fine writing instrument companies around the world are struggling—and there lies the great opportunity. In times of crisis, there is always great opportunity.

I trust my many associates at the United States Postal Service to figure out how to stay afloat in these challenging times. I first became involved closely with the USPS in 2006 when I was asked by Roy Betts, Senior Public Relations Representative, to speak of my love for Cloth Envelopes created by Rose Scharmen of Traverse City, Michigan, at the annual Postal Forum in Orlando, Florida. I was happy to share my thoughts share with an audience of 6,000 at the forum, which is a tradeshow designed to educate mail professionals, introduce new technologies and products, and most importantly interact with postal executives. I have taken advantage of these opportunities many times.

It was also a great honor to be asked by the USPS to attend the Ellen DeGeneres Show in May 2010 for the unveiling of the Animal Rescue: Adopt a Shelter Pet series of U.S. Postal commemorative stamps. Ellen unveiled the 44-cent stamps featuring the adorable faces of five dogs and five cats, all of which had been adopted from animal shelters and rescue groups.

I am now on a crusade to have a postage stamp created for the late Bil Keane, creator of the Family Circus comic. He gave my family so many Sunday mornings of joy as we would share his humor. I hope it will be a great reminder of simple all-American values, of family, of fun—all the things Bil Keane tried to create for so many. Hopefully, by the time you read this, the stamp has been approved and created.

My friends at the USPS in Washington, D.C., are long used to me calling with what I like to call my "creative" ideas to help postal workers. They have contributed so much to our society, it is my hope they get the recognition they so deserve.

Then there are the stationery industry and the Greeting Card Association—what obstacles *they* have before them with the ever-exploding Internet and digital methods of communication. I will be eternally grateful to them for introducing me to two of my dearest friends, Mike Oleskow and Russ Haan. I recall when I got the idea to create Writing In Style, I called the Greeting Card Association and asked if there was someone with whom I could talk about my idea. They said, "Why, yes, two of the most knowledgeable, greatest guys live right there in Phoenix."

I looked over their website and found it intriguing. "Are you looking for a way to grow or start a stationery business?" it read. "Let us help. One of our founders works as a consultant in this industry and can help you develop your business plan, manage finances, select sales reps, prepare for trade show, market, license and more! E-mail or call Mike Oleskow at Modus Operandi Consulting to find out more." Of course I would call!

Mike Oleskow was kind enough to meet with me and listen to my ideas about the creation of Writing In Style. He was generous in his feedback, gave support from the very beginning, and to this very day we have traveled cross country attending many conferences to advance the awareness of the handwritten note. He has dedicated hours, days, months, years, of his life to advance numerous charitable organizations. Russ has done the same. If one is fortunate to know them…well, one is fortunate indeed.

More importantly, Mike has been a dear friend to me in more ways than I could ever mention. He went to every court hearing with me, sitting for hours waiting to hear the results. He has guided me as a mother, as a friend, as a woman. Yes, he was the friend that sat with me in New York in the hotel room at the Stationery Show drinking martinis while a private detective investigated my husband. There are not enough pages in this book to express my love for him.

Of course, there's also the fine writing instrument industry. I was flattered to become a part of the PenWorld magazine when first they asked to interview me, this odd woman of interest who loves handwritten notes. I was further honored when I was asked by Glen and Susan Bowen to write a column for the magazine. It was one of the harder things I would have to give up, writing the column, when I had to leave Writing In Style behind for a couple of years during some very tumultuous times.

I am extraordinarily grateful that when I called editors Susan Bowen and Laura Chandler back, explained the last couple of years, and asked if they had a place for my writing, they welcomed me back in the Pen World magazine family. It is an absolute delight and honor to put pen to paper to create an article for this publication. I am very grateful for those who have found my columns interesting and have taken the time to write me.

Yes, there are opportunities before all of us: the United States Postal Service, the Greeting Card Association, the fine writing instrument industry. The best is yet to come, I just know it! The best is in the stories of handwritten notes. That's what I do, that is my passion: to collect and share stories about the handwritten note.

I am well aware of what stories of my life people prefer to read and talk about. I know what stories delight and mortify my audiences, my readers. I realize the more dramatic the point, the more it captures one's attention.

Honestly, though, to me it is the simple stories, the simple moments, that are the absolute best.

A Woman of Interest

I have a note written by my friend, Mladenka Zovko. Mladenka is from Croatia. She has been my friend since the day I met her. English and writing are not her strengths, though she will try anything I ask of her. She has helped me with my family and my home for many, many years. More importantly, she has been my dear friend. I remember the first time I gave her personalized stationery with her name on it. Mladenka being an uncommon name, it was the first time she had ever seen it on customized stationery. It brought tears to her eyes. To my way of thinking, personalized stationery is one of the best gifts in the world. Mladenka wrote me a simple note, "Thank You So Much." While she doesn't think her handwriting is perfect, to me the words, the writing, the effort are priceless. She wrote for me, to me. Thank you, Mladenka, for everything you have done for me. We are soul sisters.

But then there are the stories that are always crowd pleasers. One of the best involved Michael Jordan. I love this story because in my mind it captures my family perfectly. As you know, we lived in Chicago for many years—Highland Park, Lake Zurich, and Glenview, to be exact. We enjoyed Chicago as a town: the sports, the restaurants, the culture, our friends, and our careers, although the weather was awful. No matter how we tried to make the best of it, I longed to be back in Phoenix and the warm weather. We had bought a second home in Scottsdale and traveled back and forth while the kids were young. But as they got older and were in school, it was getting more difficult to go back and forth.

As I've shared with you, Paul was very involved in the sports world. The Chicago Bulls worked out at one of the facilities under his umbrella, the Caremark Deerfield Multiplex Fitness Club. Michael Palmieri was the facility manager and a close friend. In fact, one year he had gathered all of the signatures of the players on a basketball as a gift for Paul. There is a point to these details!

The Chicago Bulls had just won a great series. Michael Jordan was retiring. It was an electrifying time in Chicago. Michael Jordan was at the supposed end of his career. Paul and I were beginning our usual summer travels. He traveled for business. I would take the kids to various places around the country. He would join us whenever possible. We loved our summer travels.

The children and I had headed to Laguna Beach in California, staying at the Ritz Carlton. Laguna Beach was one of our preferred places; we went there frequently. After a morning at the beach, I had checked the kids into the kid camp program and headed to downtown for shopping and lunch.

After my favorite espresso martini and lunch at 230 Forest Avenue Restaurant and Bar, one of our favorite spots, I meandered around town, ending up in a cigar shop. I loved to surprise Paul with nice things that he enjoyed. He always enjoyed the expensive cigars I bought for him, though I wished he didn't smoke. He liked splurging and shopping for me as well. Anyway, I was in the store chatting with the owner, having a delightful afternoon. I mentioned I was staying at the Ritz Carlton. He asked if I knew Michael Jordan was coming in the next day. I admitted I didn't know that, and asked if he was sure. Yes, he knew for sure, because his limo driver had just been in to buy cigars for him. Seems they had chatted, too.

You may recall that in Game 6 of the 1998 NBA finals, Jordan scored 45 points and had the game-winning shot, one that was immortalized around the world. It was just a few days later that we would cross paths in Laguna Beach, California, at the Ritz Carlton.

I have no idea how or why I got so excited or determined, but I wanted the kids to get to say thank you to Michael Jordan for the years of entertainment he had given our family. I returned to the hotel, asked to extend our stay, and be moved to the VIP floor. Unfortunately, the hotel was fully booked, so we would need to check out as planned. I asked to be put on a wait list, which we were.

Meanwhile, I called Paul and asked him to come out to Laguna Beach. This was going to be so much fun! He was hesitant. We already had plans in place for him to come out a few days later, he had something he needed to attend to, and he could see Michael

A Woman of Interest

Jordan at the Caremark Deerfield Multiplex Fitness Club most any time he wanted. Without much effort, I convinced him to fly out early. This is the Paul Zimmermann, the real Paul Zimmermann. This is how he treated his family and me. He wanted us to be happy. He delighted in spoiling us.

Now I *really* needed that hotel room! I called the reservation manager and asked again about the room. She told me, "No, nothing had opened up." Then all of a sudden on her screen a vacancy appeared. She said, "This is unbelievable, we just got an opening on the VIP floor." I thought, "No, it's not unbelievable—it is how the universe works."

I moved our children and our things to our new room. I was known for trying to incorporate some type of an educational experience in most everything our family did. This would be no different. This would be deductive reasoning! Some would laugh and say it sounded more like stalking, but whatever—we were having fun.

The kids and I watched as people went into their rooms, marking it off if an older person went into a room; surely, this wouldn't be the room in which Michael Jordan would stay. Finally, we deduced he was staying in the Presidential Suite—a real detective agency we were!

Paul had arrived. We were having fun as a family. Like all charismatic people, the energy changes in a room on a floor when they arrive. It became obvious Michael Jordan was headed up on the elevator to the VIP floor to his suite. Maybe the large ice bucket with numerous champagne bottles being ushered in his room was a clue; maybe it was the security team speaking into their mikes. Who knows, but it was no surprise when Michael Jordan got off the elevator. I was standing at the end of the hallway, we locked eyes for a moment, nodded to each other, and he and his friends went on to his suite.

I rushed back to our room, telling my family he had arrived. Now was the time for the boys to go tell him thank you for his years of entertainment. Michelle was a just a young girl at the time.

The boys went up to the suite door, knocked and waited. Finally, the door opened. It was a security guard or friend. But the boys said what they had been practicing, "We'd like to thank Michael Jordan for entertaining our family." The man at the door politely said, "Michael is busy, not today, boys."

They came back to our room downtrodden and a little upset with me. After all this detective work, they felt it had been kind of a waste of time. I said, "Wait, we aren't done. Don't give up so easily. We'll handwrite a note to him and put it under his door."

And that's what they did. Each of my sons wrote the superstar Michael Jordan two of the sweetest, endearing handwritten notes. Fortunately, Paul, as always, had the kids' school pictures in his wallet. Each of the boys put their photo with their letter and pushed it under Michael Jordan's suite door. Fortunately, I had thought to go down to the front desk and have a copy of their handwritten notes made. I have those copies to this day.

We all went to bed. The next morning, I slept in. Paul took the kids to the concierge breakfast area to eat. Again, a common pattern: I don't generally eat breakfast, and I was probably worn out from all this Nancy Drew work!

As they were eating breakfast, Michael and his entourage came through the concierge area. He handed an envelope to the concierge, pointed at the boys, got on the elevator, and left. He stayed at the Ritz Carlton for less than 24 hours. Everyone in the room, probably 40 or so people, wanted to know how they knew him, why he pointed to them.

In the envelope he had left both of their school pictures and signed the back of them.

It is absolutely one of my favorite family stories. It depicts each of our personalities and of course the power of the handwritten note.

Paul thought maybe I would be upset about missing the experience. I assured him that I didn't miss the experience at all.

The experience was having my family come rushing back to our room, jumping in my bed saying, "We did it!"

That, my friend, is our family: Paul, Cindy, Joe, Kevin, and Michelle. If you believe anything differently, than you simply don't know us.

I'm proud of what I've accomplished thus far with Writing In Style, and it is by no means over. I created a DVD called "Sincerely Yours," enlisting the help of Crash Addams off of Craig's List, and he came to understand what I was trying to create. He understood I believed since so many people wanted to watch something or be entertained, that if I created a DVD, maybe that would be a way to get everyone to handwrite notes again, or at least have a documentary of what handwritten notes used to be. Crash helped me create the screenplay for the DVD, found the actors, shot the scenes, and edited the material. I hosted a screening party at Farrelli's Cinema Supper Club. Wendy and Tom Farrelli held a great event for me. Friends and family came to the viewing. The "Sincerely Yours" DVD was reported on in many publications.

There was also the Writing In Style Family Celebration...a family event with the intention of bringing written communication back to our community. We created fun, interactive writing adventures for people of all ages to experience the value of handwritten communication. I reached out to friends and colleagues in the community, asking them if they would participate. PenWorld International Magazine and Sheaffer USA agreed to help sponsor the event.

Glen Bowen, the original founder and publisher of Pen World International magazine, met with students and accepted single-page handwritten essays entitled "Fountain Pen," with the winning essay to be published in the magazine. How exciting for these young people! Sheaffer not only donated financially to the event, they also provided fountain pens for attendees to be able to have a first-hand experience writing with a fountain pen. Until this event, some never knew there *was* such a thing as a fountain pen.

Shea Stanfield, long known for her expertise in childhood learning, art teaching, and calligraphy, helped participants experiment with calligraphy using those fountain pens. Calligraphy can help curb attention-deficit disorder, and Shea always had her students start each day with ten minutes of calligraphy writing.

Novelist Edward "Ted" Gushee, author of "Kira's Diary" and other books, led a wonderful exercise where participants were blindfolded as he read aloud the description of colors. You would have to meet Ted to understand how magical it was. He has this booming, expressive voice. It was just pure joy to listen to him read aloud and describe colors…just magical. It was a great lesson in sensory building.

Irene Levitt, internationally renowned certified Master Graphoanalyst, shared tips on the secrets of analyzing one's handwriting. With her experiences as a lecturer for the Princess and Cunard Cruise Ships, she was a natural hit.

Anthony Turchetta of Pen Works demonstrated pen turning on a lathe. Imagine, he brought his machinery, set it up, and shared his talent of fine-tuning the creation of a pen.

Lilia Fallgatter, author of "The Most Important Letter You Will Ever Write, How to Tell Loved Ones How You Feel – Before It's Too Late," shared ways to trigger special memories and get one's thoughts on paper.

The Signature Gallery Walk was another success. I asked favors of well-known local celebrities to write a message in their own writing. I had the writings framed, with the signatures concealed. Participants had to guess who wrote the message. The first correct guess would get the donated writings. I wanted the attendees to see the personal, unique, and expressive handwriting by people from all walks of life. To my delight, every person I asked to write a message took the time to do so. Scottsdale mayor Mary Manross; Mark Tarbell, an internationally respected celebrity chef; Katie Pushor, the Director of the Arizona Lottery at the time; Robert Kiyosaki, author and founder of "Rich Dad, Poor Dad;" the Phoenix Suns

A Woman of Interest

Gorilla mascot, then Arizona Governor Janet Napolitano; Maricopa County Sheriff Joe Arpaio; renowned cardiovascular surgeon Edward B. Diethrich, MD; Phoenix Symphony conductor Michael Christie; and finally, Harvey Mackay of the Mackay Envelope Company. Mayor Mary Manross even agreed to attend and kick off the event. I was thrilled with the attendance of over 300 people and the resulting press coverage.

Oh, I suppose I must at some point get back to the very first question you asked me in this book, about the men in my life! Seriously, Ken? I either know how to pick them or really don't have a clue. I've loved all my men so much. Maybe that was the problem; I loved too much, not enough, who knows. But certainly I have loved.

For some reason, others are more interested in there being a man in my life than I am. I don't know if it is society's love of people being "in" relationships/marriages or if my being single makes my friends and family nervous! It does seem that perhaps steady relationships calm one down. Truth be told, I don't want to calm down ever again.

I haven't explored dating sites or really any of the new dating norms. Being 54 and married for so long, the dating world is different, I guess. To the best of my recollection, I haven't been on a "date" where someone comes and picks me up and takes me somewhere and pays for me and we are committed to each other exclusively. Do people still do that?

I don't know. I have been blessed with many wonderful friendships with men in my life. For this I am grateful. People tend to get the impression that I am in love or having relations or whatever with a lot of men I talk about or interact with. Since I tend to be physically and verbally affectionate, I guess this gives that impression. It doesn't bother me. I've come to learn for some reason people like to spend a lot of time talking about who is sleeping with who, or when, or how, or how often, or how not often.

It is an interesting question, all of this man/woman stuff. How am I doing? Have I avoided your question? I'm giggling again… after all, I *did* get you to read an entire book and still didn't answer your question directly! It's not wise to kiss and tell. I'm certainly not going to start now!

In truth, a serious relationship with romantic inclinations is the last thing on my mind. I have had many other, more pressing, issues to address; most importantly, the final years of parenting my children, especially my daughter in her final years at home, as I am her female role model. (Did I just write that?)

It has been important to me that after all she has been through that I protect her from watching her mother stumble through man after man or dating or whatever one wants to call it. It has been important to me that I protect her as much as I can from inappropriate sexual advances. My daughter and I have talked about this many times. We call it kitchen floor time. We sit on the kitchen floor and talk. She has thanked me for not parading men in and out of our home, our lives. It was the least I could do for her and for myself.

The truth of the matter is men and I have had interesting times, Ken. I don't really understand why. I love men. I lettered in high school as the baseball manager. I was in the locker room often. So it would seem I would have a rather good understanding of the opposite sex. I enjoy their company, am not offended by their sometime off-colored banter, and overall have a great time with them. But somehow…well, let's just say it's been interesting.

You ask Ken, how does it end? How does "The Woman of Interest" end? I don't know. I don't know when or how. I do believe the best is before me. I always believe that. But it will end with a greatness you cannot imagine. Paul and I would have it no other way. It may not end until the day I die. It may end tomorrow. One just never knows. Actually, I do know it ends the moment we let it end. The moment we are at peace.

And I am at peace. Living in the moment, being grateful for those in this particular moment in my life. And if you are reading

A Woman of Interest

this book, then you have become a part of my life, my legacy, my life story. My life story is about keeping on and keeping on, no matter the odds. It has been this way for a long, long time.

How are the kids doing? Thinking of them makes me think of more people to thank—all of the wonderful teachers and coaches who guided my children. I was very involved in the schools the kids attended. I enjoyed being the room mother, the art masterpiece mother. I enjoyed giving gifts to the teachers, thanking them for educating my children.

As for the children, they are learning. Somehow, in some way, by the grace of God, they are doing very, very well. For this I am eternally grateful. I have shared with you before, but it bears repeating: no matter what, I am most grateful that Tommy Sullivan did not harm my children. I don't care if I ever get another single blessing in my life—this alone makes me grateful beyond belief.

Unfortunately, this is not an exaggeration on my part. Not an obsessive mother making graphs and charts to create drama. The truth is, my children were in harm's way. I don't care what is ever done to me, said about me, written about me, taken from me, *anything*—at the end of every single day this is the greatest blessing I have. Secondly, I am grateful, so *very* grateful, that my children are doing well.

Hillary Clinton had it right. It takes a village. Not just any village, but the dear friends and family, the professionals, the teachers, anyone and everyone who helped me raise my children in these past years. For this, I am eternally grateful.

As you know, Ken, this is the reason I write. It is important to me that those that have helped me and helped my family know how very, very grateful I am for their help. I have no idea if this is the kind of writing that makes for a bestseller. Frankly, I don't really care.

What I *do* care about is that those acts of kindness do not go without my recognition of sincere gratitude. The acts are worthy of more than a simple thank-you note, even if it is handwritten.

Wow! That's some statement coming from a handwritten note "evangelist" like myself, isn't it?

In the darkest of moments, when there seemed to be no answer, sitting in the rubble...to those who sat with me, lent a helping hand, helped me laugh, wiped a tear, encouraged me, walked with me, shared anything and everything, poured me a glass of wine, poured me another glass of wine...for you this book is written. I am so very, very grateful.

It is my hope that every time you see a sprig of rosemary it will remind you of friendship, for that is what rosemary symbolizes, the remembrance of friendship. I've always been grateful for my friends. When I chose the rosemary sprig for the brand of my company, Writing In Style, in 2005, little did I know how perfect and dear that symbol would become for me.

To my way of thinking, in every moment, every action, every reaction we have a choice. We have a choice to extend kindness, kick someone when they are down, or act nonchalant to their cares. We make a decision if we are going to pass judgment on the rights or the wrongs of their ways. Who's to say what is right and what is wrong? I am blessed there were so many that extended kindness to me and my children. I am blessed that not everyone judged me harshly.

It was my intention to guide my children through and out of the nightmare with a sense of well-being that we could all again survive and, yes, thrive. I know for certain the best is yet to come. I wrote it once and it bears repeating.

It was important to me that my children and I focused on things bigger than us. Someone always has it worse than we do. It has always been important to me to show my gratitude and appreciation for my many blessings. I think this has been one of my saving graces.

Just the other day, my daughter shared with me that it must be genetic, this "getting signs from the universe" thing. She was in her car thinking about all she had accomplished, thinking about how proud her father would be of her. Yet, he wasn't here to share it. A song came on the radio in her car: "Daddy's Little Girl." She knew intuitively that it was a sign from her father; that he did indeed know and was proud of her.

I am grateful that she came to me and shared this story. I am grateful we listened to the song together and cried together. I can only imagine her pain. Yet somehow she has managed to put one foot in front of the other. Not only has she survived, but thrived, and so have my sons. It's an overused cliché, but in their case, well deserved.

My daughter teases me that I am like a child. She says, "Mom, you are constantly looking around like a four-year-old. Your eyes get big and you are so curious. I have to take your hand and say come along, let's go." Aren't I lucky to have a daughter that will take my hand, making sure I don't get left behind?

I feel the same for her and for my sons. We will not leave each other behind. We all have to survive and move forward. Whatever that survival and forward looks like. It will surely be different for each of us and will change as time marches on. But for this time, this moment, this is where I am and where the book must end.

I hope by sharing the various ways my friends and family have helped me, two things have occurred. One, they know how grateful I am for their support. Two, you, my reader, have maybe been given an idea of how to reach out to someone who is in need. Obviously, my preference is for you to handwrite a note, something that can be read over and over again, any time of the day, for years to come. Though I must admit the conversations, the listening, the gentle touches, the hugs, were very important, too. It always gets back to the hugs, doesn't it, Ken? Human touch, the gift of a hug.

So until next we meet, hugs and more hugs,
your friend, Cindy

ABOUT THE AUTHOR

Cindy Zimmermann was born in Kansas City and holds an undergraduate degree in marketing from Roosevelt University in Chicago, Illinois. She is a contributing columnist at *Pen World* magazine, where she writes of her love for the handwritten note. As founder of Writing in Style, and "self-appointed handwritten note advocate" she travels the world speaking about the secrets and power of the written word. She lives in her beloved casita in Paradise Valley, Arizona. www.awomanofinterest.com